Shattered by Suicide, Renewed by Resilience

Shattered by Suicide, Renewed by Resilience

How to move forward after being left behind

Jason Holzer

Dedication

To my mother and sisters, thank you for your strength and willingness to never give up. The loss of Dad was devastating, but it did not define us. I am so thankful for what we now have.

To my Holzer family of Wardsville and Wekenborg family of Taos. Thank you for your continuous love and support. I may have lost my father but you also lost a son, brother, brother-in-law, uncle and dear friend.

Preface

This book is for those who feel like no one loves them, and who think no one will care if they are gone. Nothing could be further from the truth; in fact, it is the biggest lie anyone could ever tell themselves. Suicide doesn't end the chances of life getting worse. Instead, it removes the opportunity for life to ever improve.

The shattering effects of suicide go on for decades for the loved ones who have had to move forward after being left behind. Maybe you have had feelings of loneliness or felt a lack of worth. I know I have felt like that at times in my life. However, here is the truth. Someone deeply loves you, cares about you, and values your presence. Amazingly, an even greater truth is that you have something to give that this world needs. The hard times will pass, and happiness is closer than you think. Part of my true goal for you as you read this book is that you find a greater sense of value in your life and who you are.

Every morning when you look in the mirror, smile. Simply tell yourself these words, "I love you" even when you don't feel like it. Today and every day, focus on getting 1% better at fully accepting all of who you are. If you do that, in one year alone, you will be a much improved and happier person.

There is no one else like you, and there will never be anyone else like you again. How awesome is that?! You have been gifted with amazing qualities and if you can learn how to use them, you can be unstoppable. You can make the impossible possible! You can come from nothing and have everything! The key is to only think of how you can do it and dismiss all doubt.

Some of the things I have just told you may still seem out of reach, but with this book, I want to show you what I mean. I want to show you through my own, personal story because I have lived all of this. This book tells the story of my own life and how I had to push forward after my father's suicide. It chronicles how I picked up the shattered pieces of my broken heart. It shows how I kept faith even through my own feelings of abandonment, anger, apathy, negative self-image and worthlessness. I describe my journey of how I turned it all around and create a life that continues to get better every day.

To those who are going through where I have been or to those who are trying to find clarity in their own tragedy, you just take one step at a time. Breathe, feel, grieve, but believe and have faith that better days are on their way. Whatever you do, keep moving forward and find those who you can lean on for support.

Table of Contents

Chapter 1: From Past to Present 1

Chapter 2: May 6

Chapter 3: The Drive..12

Chapter 4: The Sit-Down..17

Chapter 5: Here Today, Gone Tomorrow 21

Chapter 6: Rendezvous with Apathy..26

Chapter 7: The First Goodbye 30

Chapter 8: The Final Farewell 37

Chapter 9: Elderly Advice..43

Chapter 10: Year One...47

Chapter 11: Phenomenal Family..52

Chapter 12: Flipping the Script 58

Piece 1: First, You Love You 67

Piece 2: Faith Over Fear 74

Piece 3: Gratitude 80

Piece 4: Comfortable with Uncomfortable 84

Piece 5: Self-Discipline Over Self-Distraction 89

Piece 6: Expression Over Suppression 95

Piece 7: Empathy Instead of Sympathy 100

Piece 8: Presence Over Presents 105

Piece 9: Action Over Work 111

Piece 10: Prayer: A Balance of Moving Feet and Folded Hands 116

Piece 11: Living in Balance with God 121

Piece 12: Growth Over Fixed 125

Piece 13: A Woman's Influence 130

Piece 14: Victims Lose and Winners Choose 136

Piece 15: Autopilot Good Choices 140

A Crescendo of Joy and Thankfulness 145

Chapter 1: From Past to Present

Growing up in Taos, Missouri, I was fortunate to spend 17 incredible years with my dad. He was my first coach on the baseball field, my first teacher and, most importantly, my first role model. He was always willing to take interest in things I loved. One of my favorite things to do as a kid was playing "pitch and catch." Sometimes we called it "pitch and fetch" because there was a whole lot of throwing, a ton of fetching, but not a whole lot of catching during some of our sessions. I have many similar and fond memories of him that I will always reach for when I think of his life. I always try to focus on the good times, even on the most difficult days.

He did all the things a good father would do. He taught me how to fish, plant a garden, drive a car, and took me to all kinds of exciting events. He gave his family his best every day. The most important thing he did was teach me the right way to do things. He taught me to never take shortcuts and to put my best effort forward, no matter if I wanted to do the task at hand or not. This is a concept that I am still working on getting better at, but I thank him for ingraining that into my mind.

I am not sure I would have the courage to write this book if it wasn't for my dad's example during his lifetime. I am forever grateful for the talents he passed on to my sisters and me. After his passing, it took me 16 years to process all the good things he did for me and my family; his suicide left a wound so deep that it took me a long time to heal.

It wasn't until my 34th birthday that I had an experience so impactful, it made me ready to welcome his spiritual presence in my life again. The day before, I had listened to a podcast from Neale Donald Walsch, who wrote *Conversations with God*, and at the end he asked a profound question. He said to always be ready to ask yourself, "What does this have to do with the agenda of my soul?" I wrestled with that question all day and as I was putting my son down to sleep that night, I felt a tightness next to my heart. It felt as if I was super stressed, and it was a feeling I hadn't felt in a very long time. I very rarely get stressed and thought it was simply because I had watched my 3-month-old all day and then my 3-year-old took two hours to go to sleep.

The following morning, which was my 34th birthday, I realized what it was. After I finished my run, I felt this release of tension and I realized it was all the suppressed emotions that I had buried for years. Then for the first time since I was 17, I had a deeply spiritual conversation with my dad. Now bear in mind, I'd be lying if I said I wasn't a little freaked out initially, but then a sense of calmness and reassurance came over me and it was like a normal conversation. I sat in a chair, looked up at the sky and a sudden urge to empathize with my father washed over me.

Me: Dad, I'm so sorry.

Dad: It is ok, I'm sorry too.

Me: I wish I would have known.

Dad: No one knew, it happened within days. Look at Jenna's First Communion photo just a few days before.

Me: You were fine then?

Dad: Yes, I was.

Me: What happened? What changed within those three days?

Dad: Supervisors overwhelmed me. I felt like I couldn't keep up. I couldn't do the quality work I was accustomed to. I tried to please everyone else and I lost myself.

Me: I forgive you, Dad. I miss you so much. We all do, but I see you in my kids and in my sister's kids. Are you in a good place?

Dad: I am with God, and God is with you; thus, I am with you in spirit.

Me: I love you Dad, thank you for the time we did have together. I remember it so well.

Dad: I love you too, son. Give your boys the best damn life possible. Kickass every day and learn from me. People's approval means nothing without your own approval of yourself.

Me: Thanks, Dad… I'll remember that.

Dad: Happy Birthday son, this will be your defining year. Blow the roof off, dipshit and tell your mother, I love her.

Me: I will tell her. This is going in my book and I'll be sure she knows. Talk soon, Dad!

Dad: Later son, P.S. great job snagging in Mary. How the hell did you pull that off?

Me: It's that Holzer charm.

Dad: Pass it on to Lou and Noah.

My dad really had a way with words, and "dipshit" was a playful term he would use with me when I couldn't find something that was literally right in front of me. I never took it as demeaning or degrading, it was more humorous than anything because I would say I couldn't find something, and it would literally be right before my eyes. I still have moments like that today, and my toddler does the same thing! My wife laughs and rolls her eyes every time it happens. There is a saying in the education world that "the apple doesn't fall far from the tree" and it is absolutely true in our case!

I can't tell you how relieved I felt after that conversation. At that point in my life, I'd done a lot of praying and asking God for the ability to forgive many times, but I could feel myself unintentionally holding on to some resentment. Finally, I found peace and clarity with his passing, and I released mental blocks that had been holding me back. It was true; I needed to understand his situation. I was able to tap into my intuition and see my dad's perspective and then understand that I was also made for greatness. God created me to make a substantial difference in the world around me. My mission became clear: I wanted to start the path of reversing mental illness and teaching people how to control their minds, thoughts, and actions so they can find their own greatness.

The book starts by taking you into depths my valley and how, literally overnight, my life felt shattered, broken and ripped to pieces. Don't worry though, I am not going to keep you there. Instead, I am going to take you with me as I climbed out of my valley and up to my mountain top. After you finish the last page, my hope is to encourage you to start climbing as well. I want to leave you with a feeling that you too can pull yourself out of your valley and get to the top your mountain.

Chapter 2: May

The month of May always seems to hold a lot of opportunities for celebrating and May 2003 was no different. There were many exciting things going on. A few of my cousins were graduating, my youngest sister was making her first communion, and I was about to start a new job detailing cars, which meant I would get to test drive nearly every Mustang on the car lot that summer. I was two weeks away from finishing my junior year, about to turn 18, and starting to think about how much fun I was going to have during that summer.

I had so much to be thankful for, and I felt like my life was on cruise control. My family and I were healthy, and I was getting ready to enter adulthood with college right around the corner. I had made an amazing group of friends, many of which I still keep in contact with to this day. I was also involved in Young Life which introduced me to Jeff and Tim, two men that

I will be forever grateful for. Without them, I don't know where I would be today. Everything in life seemed to be going perfectly.

That May was supposed to be filled with scheduling college visits to take during the summer, traveling down to the lake, or going on vacation with my family. I couldn't wait for school to get out so I could start making memories with friends and family that would last a lifetime. I had no doubt in my mind it was going to be a time where we were going to get the chance to really bond as a family and grow closer to each other. In some ways, I was right. Memories were made during that particular May and the months to follow. My mom, sisters and I would have many chances grow closer as a family, but not in the way I had thought or hoped it would happen. Unfortunately, and unexpectedly for our family, my dad decided to choose a different path. A path that would shatter our hearts into pieces of immense pain and confusion. On top of that, we were left with a question that had no answer... Why?

Everyone has dates on the calendar that they always remember. December 25th is Christmas; July 4th is Independence Day; everyone recalls where they were when 9/11 happened. Then there are dates that you never forget because they change the course of your life forever.

May 8, 2003 is that day for me. It is the day my dad passed away from suicide. From my teenage perspective, everything with my dad seemed as if it was going well. However, I didn't know what was really going on in his mind, and how could I? There is really no way of knowing what another person is truly thinking. I still thought of my dad as Superman and that nothing could ever get in his way. He was a phenomenal at his craft as an electrician and everything he did, he made better. All anyone would have to do is look at my pinewood derby car from Boy Scouts and they could see how everything he touched got an upgrade.

He was a true craftsman, and he knew what high quality work looked like. He also knew how to give back to the community and how to help others. It all seemed well and good on the outside, but what I couldn't see on the inside was a darkness that clouded his logic. An invasive and instant darkness that he couldn't escape; this ominous darkness told him that this life wasn't worth living. I just wish he knew how much I loved him and how much his family loved him. Maybe he did know, but I probably could have told him more that I loved him and cared about him. Those are two things you can never tell someone enough. As I look back, I can't help but wonder if he felt like he was being taken for granted either by his job or his family. Did he feel like he had to do it all? What was the tipping point to make him feel this way? If only I had the chance to ask him, maybe we could have got him the help he needed.

I'd like to say that May 8, 2003 started like any other day, but that was simply not the case. I woke up, went to the kitchen to get breakfast and saw my mom visibly upset. She claimed she was feeling ill and had a very bad stomachache. She then told me and my sister, who was also in high school, to hurry up and get to school. "I don't want you to be late!" she said. It was that moment that I knew something wasn't right. I felt it within me. It was something I had never felt in my entire life; It was the feeling of knowing something internally before being told externally.

I wondered, "Why is she rushing us out of the house? It's only 6:45! I have a whole hour until classes start." My mom also asked me if could drop my youngest sister off at school, who was just 8 at the time. That only increased my feeling of uneasiness because I hardly ever took her to school. My mom always took her since she was able to stay home with us kids.

My mom was and still is tough as nails. Something like a little stomachache never upset her to the point of shedding tears. Nevertheless, I decided not to question her, and I just did what she asked because she did seem like she was in a lot of discomfort. I got my youngest sister to her 2nd-grade class, and then my other sister and I headed off to high school, both of us thinking that hopefully some rest would help her feel better.

On the drive into school, I asked my sister if she had seen Dad that morning, because I hadn't. She responded, saying that she hadn't seen him that morning either. Her response sent that same feeling of uneasiness sweeping over me even more. It wasn't necessarily uncommon for him to be gone for work before we got up because there were times when he'd have a longer drive to job sites and would have to leave earlier in the morning. That didn't happen very often, though, and most of the time he left for work about the same time we left to go to school.

The only thing that felt normal that day was the first part of the school day. I went to my first two classes and then headed to Algebra II/Trig for a big test right before finals. I already had an uneasy feeling about what was going on at home, and I was battling the nerves of a big test. Needless to say, my stomach felt like one big knot. As I walked into 3rd hour, the teacher immediately handed out the test so that we would have enough time to finish within the class period. I was about finished with my test and was feeling pretty good about how it was going. As I was working diligently to finish, the secretary called me to the office over the intercom. I didn't have an appointment, and I wasn't expecting anyone to meet me at school. I asked myself, "What could this possibly be about?"

My math teacher, Mr. Schaeffer, asked if the interruption could wait; his biggest pet peeve was students leaving for anything during his class. The school secretary responded by stating I needed to come to the office immediately. Chills ran rapidly through my body like I had never felt before. I turned in my test and headed to the front office.

"Something's not right, what the hell is going on?" I thought to myself. I anxiously arrived at the office, and the secretary proceeded to tell me that I was going to be picked up by my aunt and uncle at any moment and to stay close. "Do I have time to go get my things?" I asked. She responded, "No, please stay here, they will be here soon to get you." I kept thinking, "Damn, I get called out of class, I can't get my things, and my aunt and uncle are picking us up from school. Can someone tell me what in the world is going on?" My mind was racing, but at the same time it felt like everything I did was in slow motion.

I knew something was wrong, and not knowing what it was exactly filled my mind with the worst thoughts. Sadly, even my worst thoughts could never have prepared me for what I was about to face.

Chapter 3: The Drive

Shortly after I stopped pacing and sat down, my aunt and uncle arrived to pick up my sister and me from the school office. They told us that Dad had been in a serious accident and they were here to bring us to the hospital. "Is he ok?" I asked. They couldn't give me much of an answer and honestly, how could they? How do you try to comfort your 17 and 15-year-old nephew and niece when you know the truth? Even though they knew, there was no way they could tell us what really was going on. It wasn't their place; they were just doing the best they could to get us home as quick as possible. God bless them for having the bravery and courage to come get us. It was something that had to be done, but I still cannot imagine how difficult of a task that must have been. They were given the duty of bringing us home to the news that our dad had passed away, but they had to tell us something was wrong with him without revealing what actually happened. Tom and Paula, thank you for your courage.

After we got in the car, we took a right turn out of school. This was the opposite way of the hospital, and it was then that I knew this was more serious than an injury. More thoughts of worst-case scenarios flooded my mind. All I could do was stare out of the car window as they drove. While I sat in the car, my emotions would constantly switch from either feeling nothing or feeling everything. There was no middle ground. In fact, I was so occupied by what was happening inside me, I couldn't even open my mouth to say, "Isn't the hospital in the other direction?" It was like someone clamped my mouth shut with vice grips. Not only did I feel like I couldn't speak, but I couldn't even look at my sister to see what she was doing. I just continued to gaze out of the car window and look at the landscape that I had driven past hundreds of times. The trees, houses, and farmland all looked the same but my life, as I had always known it, was about to look completely different. My thoughts were like a race car going at top speed and my mind was the track as I continued to go through thousands of scenarios on how my life was about to change forever.

At 17 years old, intuition can be a tricky thing. I had no understanding of why I felt the way I did. How do you explain just knowing something is true before you experience it? As far as I can remember, this was my first real intuitive experience and I wrestled with it the whole way home. I didn't want to believe what my gut was telling me. I kept lying to myself as I was trying to think positive thoughts like, "Dad's ok, he just got hurt at work, no big deal." Emotions were inundating my body as I was trying to convince myself that he was fine, even though deep down I already knew the truth. It was the ultimate paradox of thinking one thing but knowing another.

Emotions kept swirling through my body and my mind couldn't stop thinking as we continued to drive towards the house. Then, as we turned into my neighborhood, all feeling left my body and my thoughts left my mind. I felt lifeless. Immediately, it was like everything vanished from my body followed by a sharp coldness that ran up my arms. I vividly remember that they were the sharpest chills anyone could imagine; it was an out of body experience. I was about to face my worst fear.

When we turned onto my street, I glanced up and saw the street sign, St Francis Dr., in white letters with the green backdrop. This sign had always been the marker for a blissful turn for as long as I could remember. I always loved coming home and for good reason. My parents gave every effort to give us kids the best life possible. It was a home of laughter, peace, and comfort. We had our ups and downs, but it was a place I always cherished. Unfortunately, coming home this time meant I was about to step into the most devastating news of my entire life.

As we drove closer, I was able to see our house in the distance and there must have been 30 cars in the driveway and along the road. "Why are there so many cars at our house?" I thought to myself. I then recognized every vehicle belonged to a family member. As we continued to get closer, I kept thinking "If Dad is at the hospital, why is everyone here?"

As we were approaching the driveway, I felt it again, that same intuitive feeling. It was the feeling that was telling me that my father was gone. I felt the seat belt tightening as my heart started beating faster; it felt like I couldn't breathe. Life felt like a movie and once again everything went into slow motion. As my uncle parked the car, the first tear of millions surfaced in my eye. My vision blurred as it surfaced, then it ran down my cheek and landed on my pants. I needed to know this wasn't a dream. I had to feel something. My body was so numb until that tear ran down my face. The sensation of that cold tear made me realize that this was real and that this was happening. There was nothing I could do to stop it. At first, I was hesitant and didn't want to get out of the car. I didn't want to walk up to the patio and step into that house. I didn't want to know what happened. I just wanted things to go back to how they were the day before. My uncle opened my door and when I stepped out of the car, my feet felt like someone had put shackles on them. Why did every step feel so heavy? I couldn't even lift my head to see ahead of me. I just looked down at my feet as I took each step.

Jason Holzer

I could feel the build-up of emotion inside me as I got closer to the house. I tried to push it back down thinking that it would go away. I didn't want to believe what I was about to be told. Every time I suppressed an emotion, it came back stronger. As I took each step and climbed each stair, it felt like I was a volcano of emotions about to erupt, or a ticking time bomb about to explode. I got to the front door and wrapped my hand around the door handle. It was cold. It was a black door handle and it faced the east side of the house. I remember briefly wondering why the handle was cold. If anything, it should have been hot since the sun had been shining all morning. Once again, that the cold feeling rushed right through my arm to my chest. I was about to face a life altering, earth-shattering experience that no 17-year-old, or anyone else, should ever have to endure.

Chapter 4: The Sit-Down

As I stepped through the front door and walked into my home I first saw my grandma sitting on the couch in the living room. She had a box of tissues grabbing one after another. The couch faced away from me, so I couldn't see her face, but I could feel her emotion. I could feel the heaviness in the room as if someone tied a weight to my heart. There were tissues everywhere. Everyone had a box and seemed to have been in tears for hours. It felt like my whole family was looking at me as they were trying to make sense of it as well. I could feel their sadness as I looked at their faces, and I felt that same tightness in my throat that seemed to keep me speechless. What the hell did they all know that I had yet to find out? Even though my gut instinct had already told me what I didn't want to believe. The tears started to run faster. Then as I turned my head back, I saw my mother. She hadn't stopped crying since we left. She was able to choke up the words, "Jason, we need to go to your room, I have to tell you something." I never dreaded walking to my own room a single day in my life until that moment. I followed her down the hallway, feeling my feet hit the floor with every step, thoughts overtaking my mind about what I was about to hear.

I look back now and I think about how difficult that had to have been for my mom. How do you tell a 17, 15, and an 8-year-old, what she was about to tell us? She sat all three of us on the bed, knelt, and put her hand on our knees. I can still feel the pressure of her hand on my knee. Since we were sitting so close, she was able to reach all three of us at once. She took one big gulp as the tears kept pouring out of her face. She told me what I already knew, "Dad died this morning" she managed to say.

Those words felt like a dagger to my soul. I stood up and screamed, "NNNNNNNOOOOOOO!!!!" at the top of my lungs. The rage and anger intensified instantly as I became overwhelmed with adrenaline. Immediately, I walked over to my bedroom closet and started banging on one of the doors with my fists. BAM! BAM! BAM! It was as if my fists turned into sledgehammers and just started wailing. A short time later, two of my uncles ran in and had to hug me down. Even though I only weighed 140 pounds, it took two grown men to get me to calm down. They thought I was going to break my hand as hard as I kept wailing against the closet door. When they finally got me to sit down again, I asked my mom, how? Was it a car accident? A work accident? I was hoping for some natural cause, but more importantly, a reason that I could eventually accept. I was desperately hoping he did something courageous that I could take pride in. Something where people would say, "Hey, you're Alan's son! Didn't he pass away by helping someone else?" That would have been something I could have, in time, lived with and been ok with talking to others about. Unfortunately, that wasn't the case.

When my mom told us that he took his own life, all I could muster up was why? Was it me? Was I not enough for him? Anger turned to confusion, guilt, and blame. I was his only son and with everything I did, I tried to make him proud. I can say with certainty my sisters felt the same. We all loved him so much. My mind was bombarded with questions. I asked my mother if there was a note, farewell letter, or any explanation at all. There was nothing. Not one thing; I had no answers and neither did my family.

It is hard enough when someone we love and care about passes away, but then there is suicide. Suicide takes loss to a deeper and much more complex level. Death is never easy, but when someone we love takes their own life, we can't help but think that for some reason we had something to do with it. These were the thoughts that ran through my head. Did I do something or not do something? Did I disappoint him? Those questions with no answers swirled around in my head. The only person that could ever answer them was gone, and so my mom, sisters and I were left with immense confusion as we tried to fully comprehend what had just taken place.

The tragedy and reality of suicide is the ripple effect it has on those left behind. The simple question of "Why?" becomes so complex and goes forever unanswered. There is only speculation left. There was no note, no goodbye letter, no closure, absolutely nothing. The man I knew who would laugh at his own jokes, coach his kids' sports teams, work hard to support his family and, from my teenage perspective, seemed to be enjoying his life, was now forever gone.

My last memory of his life was him snoring, shirtless on the couch as I finished studying for my Algebra test, thinking that I would see him tomorrow. Well, when tomorrow came, I was still there. However, he chose not to be. I had to somehow find a way to pick up the pieces and move forward after being left behind.

Chapter 5: Here Today, Gone Tomorrow

The deep pains of my father's suicide made me realize what is true today may not be true tomorrow. It was a tough lesson to learn that there are no guarantees in life. As a 17-year-old, I thought my parents would be around forever. They were only in their early forties. I assumed and took for granted that they would always be there for me because they always had been before. I wasn't as thankful as I could have been, and I didn't understand or appreciate all the things my parents did for me until it was too late. Since my mother is still living, I express gratitude to her constantly. Her strength during such a difficult time helped us get through as our lives were flipped upside down.

Unfortunately, I waited until it was too late to thank my dad for providing for me and my family. It was too late to tell him that I loved him, and it was too late to give him a hug and say everything is going to be ok. To this day, it runs through my mind all the time. I know I can't do anything about it now, but I can't help wondering what life would be like if he was still here. However, I knew I had to stop playing the "what if" scenarios because the reality was that I could only control my actions in the present. The past is what it is, and I could learn from it, but to dwell on it would have only held me back. I did eventually get to a point where I stopped telling myself, "What if all he needed was a hug" or "What if all he needed was affirmation that he is enough?" "What if all he needed was his son to tell him, Love ya, Dad?" Instead, I started asking myself questions like, "How can I make my life better today?" and "What can I do today that will make a better tomorrow?" Now I take action because I know that life is meant to be lived to the fullest. I make the decision to be ready to gratefully give and humbly receive. This is what I believe God asks of all of us.

It seems as if many teenagers think they are too cool for their parents. I lived it myself and I see it all the time. Most of the time it is because of a lack of awareness and understanding; if they really knew how much is being provided for them, they would have a greater appreciation. The saying is very true: you don't know what you have until it's gone. I was now realizing that for the rest of my life, I would no longer have a physically present father. It was like being sideswiped and whiplashed, you don't see it coming until it's already happened. It was a time when I needed him the most. I now know the importance of having a father who is physically present and there for me, and that is my promise to my two sons. I will control everything I can to be there for them. I will take care of myself, so I can give them everything they deserve from a father, which is simply my best every day. It's what every child deserves.

"Here today and gone tomorrow" is a phrase I had heard before, but I never thought I would live it. "This wasn't supposed to be," is a thought I had over and over. Again, I reemphasize that this is when I needed my father the most as I was at the cusp of turning 18, which is when America/society claims you as an adult. What do you do as an adult? How do you succeed in this crazy world? What is my place as a man in this world? These were just a few of the questions that would surface, and I wasn't sure where I would find the answers. My time with my father was taken without warning and these types of questions I wanted to ask him were left for someone else to answer. Thank God for Tim and Jeff, two guys who were in college that chose to be Young Life leaders and be an example for teenagers in high school. God knew exactly what I needed when I needed it.

At least when we know we don't have much time with someone we can create memories, spend time with them on their last days, and say our final see ya later. We can laugh about the good times, the dumb things they did and most importantly we can say goodbye and they can say something like, "I'll be waiting for you on the other side" or even a simple "I love you." We can grieve with them, hug them, kiss them on the forehead and let them know how much they mean to us. I would have given anything for that chance. Suicide robbed me of at least getting to say goodbye, to say sorry, I love you, I'll miss you or to simply say anything at all.

I needed my father's perspective to help form my own. I needed his experiences to guide me so that I could handle adversity and figure out what to do when I didn't know what to do. Who better to understand what I may be going through than the man that raised me as a child, and knew what I struggled with and who might have had similar struggles when he was a child? Now it felt all for naught, and my mind kept racing with those thoughts. I continued to keep thinking about why he did what he did, and how could he? I was only frustrating myself because I kept asking questions that had no answers.

As I kept asking questions with no answers over and over, feelings of apathy slowly crept into my subconscious. After the initial shock, anger, and flood of grieving emotions had left my body, I simply felt nothing for weeks after we laid him to rest. I felt cold and apathetic as if someone turned on a vacuum and sucked my soul right out of my body. Maybe that explains why I slept straight through the night that first night after he was gone. I thought so much that day that my mind just shut off. I felt so much that day that my body could feel any more. I had never felt so lifeless, and it was almost as if I went into emotional shock.

I woke up the next day and my mom asked me if I got any sleep. I felt bad telling her that I slept through the night just fine. However, it did give her some relief that I did get some sleep. I needed the rest because the coming days required more energy than I could ever imagine. I'd like to say the worst day of my life was behind me, but the aftershocks would continue to be an ever-present burden. Sometimes it's not the initial earthquake that hits you the hardest, it's the aftershocks that follow that can take the biggest toll.

I never fully realized how much was involved when someone died, especially when the only death experience I had so far was a pet dying. Now was the time where we had to make appointments to arrange his visitation and funeral. Someone had to help my mom make these tough decisions that we never thought we would have to make. I think it is fair to say that we all had our minds somewhere else and to try and figure out what flowers we wanted was nearly an impossible task. These were the last things we wanted to do, but they needed to be done.

Chapter 6: Rendezvous with Apathy

The day after my father's passing felt like I was living in a dream. I hoped I would wake up and things would be like before, but that was wishful thinking. The whole day felt like everything was moving in slow motion as we made our way from one appointment to another as we prepared for Dad's visitation and funeral. The entire time I remember being overwhelmed with apathy and unable to muster up any emotion. I could not have cared less about the flowers, casket, what he would be wearing, and other arrangements that we had to decide upon. I remember thinking over and over, "What does it matter? He's gone."

I sat in a chair flipping through a catalog of fancy caskets, and asking myself, "How is this real? I am 17 and picking out my dad's casket? I should be doing this when I'm 67, not now!" I never thought in a million years that this would be my reality. I guess no one probably does. Then, the funeral home director guided us through a room filled with various types of caskets on display. Chills ran through my body as I walked into the room. "What do you all think?" He asked. "Do you like any of them?" "Is this guy serious?" I thought. I don't give a damn about any of this. The fact is my dad is going to be laying in one of these and then it is going to be buried, with him in it. "Who freaking cares what it looks like?"

It was hard enough for me to come to terms with my father being gone, and now I must to make decisions about how his funeral will look. This was like throwing salt into a deep, painful wound. I didn't care; I just wanted my dad back. I just wanted him alive. I just wanted to play catch in the backyard, shoot hoops in the driveway; I would have even taken mowing the yard for five hours. Anything, and I mean anything but this situation. Then as I looked at my mom and sisters and I realized I had to help them with these decisions. We were all hurting, and my apathetic attitude wasn't helping. We were all facing the same reality. None of us wanted to do this, but this was what we had to do. More than ever we had to stick together. More than ever we needed each other.

My mom looked at me with tears streaming down her face and said, "I need your help with this, Jason. I can't do it alone." "Please, help me, son." I gave her a big hug and said, "Ok Mom,

I will. We will get through this." She was now the only parent I had left, I had no choice but to step up and help her. It was time to roll up my sleeves and prepare myself for something no one is ever really prepared for. I hated every minute of it and the anger set in. "Why Dad?" "Why would you do this to Mom, and us kids?" I kept asking over and over. I got so angry at him and because of that became more motivated to help my mom. It was something I needed because as hard as it was for me, it was significantly more difficult for my mother. The man she loved left her with three young children. Children, who were at an age where they needed their father the most and who were now solely relying on her. More than that, she lost the man she loved more than anything.

It was at that moment I realized my mom needed me, more than ever. I needed to find a source of strength to help her get through this because she had to be strong for us as well. I asked God to give me the strength to push forward even though I just wanted to run and hide. After what felt like an unending time warp, we got all the arrangements taken care of and everything was scheduled. I looked at the time and it was only noon. Time felt like it stood still. How is it only noon? Literally, we were only there for two hours. To say these days were the longest days of my life would be an understatement. Luckily, my Uncle Sam told me he was going to take me to lunch. Initially, I didn't want to go, but then again, I didn't want to do anything. However, my mom encouraged me to go and I obliged. She had enough on her plate. The last thing she needed was an unruly teenager.

That lunch with Sam ended up being exactly what I needed. He was able to make me laugh, which was a nice relief from all the sadness, and he told me that even though this is hard right now, life will get easier with time. This type of encouragement was essential for me to hear as I was preparing to say my final goodbyes to my dad.

Chapter 7: The First Goodbye

After nearly two days of having limited to no feeling at all, it was time for me to get ready for the private visitation. This was exclusively for family on the evening before the funeral. I remember everything feeling eerie and different as I put on my dress pants, button-up, and tie. Before this, when I had been asked to dress nice it was because of a celebration like a wedding, celebrating a Sacrament, or a major holiday Mass. It was less than a week ago that we celebrated my youngest sister's First Communion, and if you look at that picture you would never have guessed what was really going through my dad's mind. You would have never guessed that was going to be our last family picture. That's what is crazy; I learned that you can perceive something to be true externally, and it could be the opposite of what's going on internally. We even looked the part of a happy family with our big smiles and being formally dressed for a big moment in my youngest sister's life. We looked like we were full of excitement and joy, and it is possible on that day that we were. At that time, if someone would have told me, in less than a week, I'd be dressing up to say my final goodbyes to my father, I would have thought they were crazy.

However, as crazy as it seemed, this was my new reality. As I buttoned up my shirt, I felt my eyes welling up with tears. Then they started to surface, and it was during that moment I knew that reality was coming full force. I kept hoping and hoping it was all just a bad dream. Unfortunately, it didn't matter how much I hoped, this was real. So, I just let the tears fall down my face. The tears tingled the tiny hairs on my cheek then ran down the side of my face and fell to the floor. I had to feel it; it was my affirmation that this was happening and that there was no way around it. This was the beginning of my family and me having to say our final goodbyes to the man we all loved the most.

I walked out of my room and I saw my mom and sisters with red faces and Kleenexes. It was all hitting us at the same time. The limo was here to chauffeur us to the funeral home. It was only one month before that I was in a limo, for my first prom, having one of the best times in my life. Now, I was in a similar, luxury vehicle with a completely different feel. As the limo driver started the car and headed towards the funeral home, all I could do was stare out the window. It felt like deja vu from just two days ago when my aunt and uncle picked us up from school. Making eye contact with anyone made me want to cry.

Up to this point, crying was something I had not done very much in my life. I think it was because crying made me feel weak, and I felt like I had to be the strong one because now I was the only man. Men must stay strong regardless, is the feeling that I always had, and crying was a sign of vulnerability and weakness. At least that is what I had come to believe somewhere along the way. I can't pinpoint exactly where I got that belief from; it was never directly taught to me. It is just the conclusion I got from my childhood. So, as the drive went on, I just looked out the window. I continued staring at the countryside, watching the wind whoosh through the trees and looking at the farmhouses as we headed into town.

Quickly, those windy country roads turned into the highway, and there was the capital building of Missouri. This was the first major sign that we were getting close and again my eyes started to well up. My mom put her hand on my knee and assured me that it was ok to cry. She assured me that holding it in would only make it worse and that letting it out will do me good. So, I let the tears fall again, it did seem to help. As the limo parked under the carport, I looked to my left and I saw the hearse. Chills rushed up through my spine and this time they stayed. It was as if my nervous system was in overdrive. "Holy shit, he's in there."

"I don't know if I can do this," I thought. I wanted to just run like Forrest Gump did in the movies. I didn't care where, just anywhere but where I was. However, I had nowhere to run, so my feet kept walking towards the double doors of the funeral chapel.

We walked in and were greeted by the funeral home director. He had a big smile on his face as he greeted us and all I could think was, "What the hell is this guy smiling about?" I realize now he was just doing his job but the last thing I wanted to hear was some stranger wishing me "best condolences" or "sympathies". He then said, "You all will get the chance to see him first as a family this evening before the public visitation tomorrow." "What an opportunity," I thought sarcastically. I didn't want to think like that but just the way he said it, made it feel like our situation was an honor or a privilege. The last thing I want VIP service for is any funeral and especially my own father's, who just took his own life and we have no clue why.

Then the funeral director opened the door, and at the other end of the room was Dad. Chills came back again, this time even more intense. We walked down the hallway, every step I took the emotion kept building and building and then expressed in the form of tears that I have never experienced before. All I could do was stare at him, and think "Dad, just wake up! Please wake up! It's me Jason, your son!" The whole time I just knelt and prayed, get up Dad, tell me this is a dream. He just stayed there. It didn't matter how much I begged and prayed, the harsh reality was that he was going to stay there. Blurred vision from tears and a feeling of weakness made it hard to even stand up. How? And Why? played in my mind like a song on repeat. God help me understand.

It was almost time to open the doors to the rest of the family and I had to stand up. I didn't want to; I just wanted to bury my head into the cushion on top of the kneeler. There are times in life where our lone option is to push through, and we must get up and keep going. That was the only option I had that day. It took a little assistance from an usher, but I got my feet underneath me, and I stood next to my mom, sisters, and my dad. As family came to pay their respects that night and then the public the following morning, I had a hard time even making eye contact with anyone. Every time I saw a friend or family member, tears just kept coming and I let it happen. I had to grieve because if I didn't then that suppressed grief would turn into anger. I didn't want to be angry. I decided that sadness was better than anger. So, I just cried. As people came by, I would choke up "thank you for coming," as the tears kept flowing. Eventually, the tears did stop but I think it was only because I physically couldn't cry anymore. I remember feeling dehydrated from the excess of tears that ran down my cheeks that night. My face looked like it was sunburned because of the endless roller coaster of emotion each visitation sent me through.

Friday evening and Saturday morning before the funeral, all I could think was, "I wish I would have given him more hugs; I wish I would have said I love you more." All the regret came to my mind about the things I wish I would have done that possibly could have made a difference. I know I said those things on occasion, but my teenage coolness and ignorance didn't understand the need or desire to tell him every day. What if he would have known how thankful I truly was, as well as how much I admired and looked up to him? Instead, I took it for granted, and I assumed that he knew. I'll never know if it would have made a difference, but I do know that it could have only helped if I had made more of an effort to be more expressive. If I would have gotten out of my comfort zone a little more, and told him how I felt about him, maybe it would have made a difference. Maybe, instead of me standing next to his eternal resting place, I would be standing next to him face to face having meaningful conversations, playing games or even just making each other laugh by telling dumb jokes.

When I got home from the family only visitation, I was still in utter disbelief about what just happened to me. I hugged my mom a little tighter that night. I started telling my sisters' I loved them, which was something I had never done before. It's not cool to tell your little sisters you love them when you're 17. I decided that cool didn't matter to me anymore, because being cool just left me with a whole lot of regret. I knew the next day was going to be the most difficult. The next day was the public visitation and the funeral. Regardless if I was ready for it or not, it was happening. No amount of preparation or training could have made me ready for a situation like this, and there was nothing I could do to stop it from happening. I just had to keep going, keep praying and keep asking for strength to push through the pain and numbness. The numbness came back as I started to fall asleep from the emotional exhaustion of the day. I remember, before I fell asleep, simply asking God for the strength to get up and get through tomorrow. When I faced the fact that there was no getting around this, all I could do was reach for faith and ask for strength and resilience.

I remember that I kept telling myself over and over, I'll tell him tomorrow or I'll ask Dad tomorrow. Well, May 8th came and for my dad, tomorrow never came and my opportunities to tell him what I was feeling or what I was questioning were also gone.

Here is the message I want everyone to understand... No one has ever regretted saying I love you or I care about you more often. We never know what someone else is going through. Maybe all someone needs is a call, text, email, or an invitation. Something as simple as that could literally change the course of a person's life. The impact of a small act of kindness can have a profound effect. Maybe even save a person's life. We just never know how much we can positively impact another. Again, simply saying kind words, making others feel included or sending message of compassion could make all the difference.

Chapter 8: The Final Farewell

I remember tossing and turning a lot the night before the funeral. Sleep was much more difficult because of the thoughts that were racing through my mind. I also felt like I was too tired to fall asleep, like a slap happy toddler after a long day of activities. The emotional and mental exhaustion seemed to have a reverse effect on my ability to rest. I laid in my bed, staring at the ceiling, watching the blades of the fan rotate, and rotate, and rotate. The feeling of cool air against my skin was a welcome feeling. However, I couldn't get out of my mind seeing my dad that way. It was real and this was no dream. Then I came to another realization that the funeral was just a short 12 hours away.

The minutes felt like hours that night. I tried to sleep, thinking that maybe sleep would help me escape the pain. It came rushing right to the core of my heart, like a flood gate being opened, as the feelings of numbness started to go away. It hurt, it was sharp, and it was a wound that hit deep in the recesses of my being. Deeper than any physical agony I had ever felt. It was like someone just ripped my heart out, and not understanding how to deal with these feelings, I pushed them down. I thought that suppressing them would help them go away. Again, all I wanted was to fall asleep and escape the pain for at least a few hours.

Eventually, I did fall asleep but before I knew it, I felt the warmth of the sun cascading into my window. It was a great feeling, a feeling of normalcy and comfort. Then my feet hit the floor and as I stood up, my conscious thought kicked in. It was the day of the funeral and it was going to be the most difficult day I had ever experienced. I walked into the kitchen and I tried to eat, but I couldn't. Anxiety filled my body and it felt as if someone dropped an anchor into my stomach. My mom tried to encourage me to eat something, we all knew we needed to eat, but it's hard when you know what's coming. It was like taking shelter before a tornado, you know it's coming and all you can do is face it and pray for God's strength to help you through.

I was able to force down some fruit and drank some water, and shortly after that, our ride arrived. "Man, here we go again," I thought, and that familiar rush of emotions came back. I got into the limo, and my eyes were already starting to blur. Tears, tears and more tears. We barely exited the driveway and I couldn't hold them back. I tried to speak but every time I tried to say something, nothing came out. I was speechless, an emotional mess and we hadn't even got to the public visitation yet. In my mind, I kept asking God to give me the strength, help me through this as we made our way to the funeral home. Little did I realize how much strength I would need. After the public visitation, we processed to church for the funeral.

When we arrived, I was the first to get out. My mom was next and as she was getting out of the car, she could barely stand. "Jason, I am so weak," she said. It was a feeling I was familiar with as well but not to the extent of my mom. Then she said, "I can't walk. I can't do this." With my sisters on one side and me on the other, we joined together as we helped our mom. She had been our rock the last few days, she needed us to help her get to the front door of the church. She was the one who had been giving us all the help we needed during this time. Now it was our turn to help her get through our final goodbye.

The bells sounded. It was 2:00. I can still feel the vibrations of the bells and I can still hear "Dong, Dong, Dong, Dong." To this day it still gives me chills when I hear church bells. It gave me such an eerie feeling as I stood at the entrance of the church, next to my mom and sisters. Right in front of me were the pallbearers, getting ready to move the casket down the aisle to the front of the church. The music started, and as Father and the servers began to walk up the aisle, we followed right behind. As we made our way forward, I could feel the heaviness in the church. It felt like there were thousands of eyes on us as we walked down the aisle. As we got about halfway, my mom's legs gave out again. "I can't do this," she said, barely able to get the words out of her mouth. I could feel the weakness in my legs as well. Emotions were so deep and so heavy; it had taken its toll on each of us. However, God gave me and my sisters the strength we needed, and we figured out a way, as we put my mom's arms around our shoulders and helped her get to our pew to take a seat.

The whole service was a blur to me. I couldn't tell you a single thing the priest said in his message. I'm sure he said a lot of great things about my dad, but all I could do was look at the casket and keep asking, "Why?" The question that had no answer consumed my mind as we went through the funeral Mass. My face still looked sunburnt from all the tears and raw emotion of this entire experience. I didn't understand what was so bad that it would coerce someone to do this. Then the final hymn resonated, and I realized we were about to proceed to the cemetery. An hour passed and even though I was there physically, mentally I was in another universe. We were able to gather the strength and walk back to get in the limo. We had no choice anyway, it's what we needed to do. There are times in life when the only path is the one that is going to drag you through the mud, but one step at a time and we were getting through it.

We stood shoulder to shoulder just holding each other as we walked out of the church. All of us wondering, how are we going to move forward without him?

We got to the cemetery and to his final resting place. I could see the mountain of dirt that had been piled up preparing his grave. I was hit with a dose of reality in that moment. It was a reminder that this physical life is temporary, and eventually it does end at some point. However, as I walked up to take my seat next to my father's headstone, I made the decision that my path would be different. Going through this experience, I knew I had to choose a different way, a better way. Still raw with emotions, I concluded that I was not going to let these moments be an excuse and my life would end on God's time, not on mine. I made a commitment to myself that no matter how long it took, I would use this pain and turn it into strength, and I would find my passion and purpose. I didn't know what that meant or what that looked like at the time, but I did know this: I didn't want to feel this depth of agony again, nor would I wish this anguish on anyone else.

As we took a seat and the priest gave his final blessing, I buried my face in my mother's shoulder. I never knew I could cry so much in two days. Once the blessing was over an usher gave us all a balloon and a sharpie to write a farewell message. I couldn't write what I really wanted to because those words dripped with anger and resentment. Somehow, I knew writing something like that would only cause more anger and resentment. So, I simply wrote, "I love you, Dad. I'll miss you, and I hope you are in Heaven." I held onto the bottom of the string and waited for everyone else to finish. Then, I let go and watched the balloon float up into the deep blue sky.

I had only one choice and that was to let myself grieve and heal this wound. I still had my life to live, and regardless of what I just went through, no one was going to feel sorry for me for too long. I had to start picking up the shattered pieces of my life and put them back into place. I knew if I had the right attitude mixed with resiliency, an amazing life was still ahead of me. That was my plan then and still is to this day. At the time, I didn't know how it would happen, I just decided to have the faith that life would get better.

Once my balloon was out of sight, I gave my mom and sisters a hug and started walking to the car to go home. I glanced over my shoulder, looked back at the headstone and understood that this is now my life. It was the start of all of us having to move forward after being left behind.

Chapter 9: Elderly Advice

After we left the cemetery, there was a meal provided for us and my extended family. I knew I had to eat but as I looked at my food nothing looked good. Not even the fried chicken, that I would normally have devoured, looked appetizing. I was able to push down a few spoonfuls of vegetables and a few bites of chicken, but my mind was so hung up on how I move my life forward after what I just experienced. Where do I even start? This was the million-dollar question, and if someone had the answer, right about now would have been a good time to reveal it to me.

The loss of my father made me feel utterly lost and bewildered. I was standing in a room with my family who cared and loved me, but I felt like I had a hard time connecting with any of them. Everything I had become accustomed to was now a memory. Simple routines like driving down St. Francis Dr. to head home would never be the same again. Dad's truck wasn't pulling into the driveway ever again. The little things, like asking him how his day was or even asking if he wanted to play catch or shoot hoops, were never going to happen again. This was my new normal. I had no choice but to get used to it, regardless of how I felt about it. Nervousness and anxiety spread through my body constantly. It felt like an invasion of negativity and paranoia because all I could think about was something bad happening again. I had to retrain myself to stop thinking in that manner and believe that there were good times coming as hard as it was to imagine at the time.

When we got home, there were still people at the house, most of them trying to help as best they could. As I walked through the living room to go talk to one of my uncles, I felt a small hand lightly grab my arm. I turned and looked; it was an old woman. I had no idea who she was, a friend of the family I assumed, or maybe a distant relative. I didn't recognize her but what she was about to tell me would spin my thoughts even more.

Her touch on my arm was gentle but the words she spoke to me, I'll never forget. She looked at me and said, "I'm sorry for your loss, but it looks like you're the man of the house now." Wait... what? What does that even mean? Man of the house? I'm not even considered an adult yet. I make $8 an hour sacking groceries, so I can put gas in my car. What the heck is this lady talking about? My father was just laid to rest, and I haven't even fully wrapped my head around what the hell just happened to my family and me. Now, I have a stranger telling me that I am the man of the house? Does she mean I am supposed to be the provider for my mom and two younger sisters? Why would she say that? "Thanks, Dad" I thought. I failed to realize that the anger and resentment kept seeping into my soul and that I was starting to play the victim role already. Without fully understanding how to cope with my emotions, I suppressed them even more. The main thing I wasn't realizing was that victims never win. Feeling sorry for myself was not going to heal my deepest wounds; instead, it would only make them worse.

That old woman may have had good intentions. Maybe she thought I would be inspired by her words or that's just the way it was when she was growing up. However, after hearing what she said, all I felt was more feelings that weren't going to help me start the healing process. I was a teenager in need of guidance and how to handle these emotions that kept overwhelming me. I didn't have a clue about what being the man of the house meant, and I definitely didn't know how to provide for a family.

Later that evening, I was talking with my mom and I asked her, "Does this mean that I am the man of the house? I don't know how to take care of a family, Mom. I am still just a kid in a lot of ways, I'm not even eighteen yet." My mom looked at me, face still red from all the tears that had been falling for days, and assured me that she was the adult and would take care of us. She told me she is just going to need me to help more.

That was the relief I needed. I didn't have to be the man of the house, just a helper of the house. That was something I could control, and I could do with confidence. I'd been expected to help around the house my entire life, but my level of responsibility would be raised. I would have to drive my sisters sometimes, especially the one in high school, which I did anyway. I would have to do more of the yard work, which again I was ok with and very capable. Those were things I was confident I could do. Even though there was now more responsibility for me, and more was expected of me, I didn't have to be a provider. The last thing my mom said to me was something I'll never forget. She said, "All we can do is take it one day at a time. There will be good days and there will be very hard days. We just have to stick together."

Our lives had been flipped upside down, but we had a choice to make. We had to give ourselves time to grieve, process it all and heal. This doesn't happen overnight; it could take days, months, years, possibly even decades in some cases. However, my mom gave me the confidence that eventually we would create our new normal and that we can each still live a great life. We would make it through this together. We would be stronger and more resilient to meet life's challenges.

Chapter 10: Year One

The first year of anything is always an adjustment, but this adjustment was going to be long and treacherous. We had two weeks of school left and we did have the option to stay home, but my mom decided that it would be best to get out and be around others. It was definitely the best thing for me to be around friends and start building a new routine. I didn't want to do it, but I needed to do it. This concept of knowing what I needed to do regardless of whether or not I wanted to was important for me to understand because I would have many more similar scenarios like this in years to come.

The first day I came back to school was all sorts of weird. It felt like everyone in the whole school knew, and when I walked the hallways, I could feel the awkward looks I was getting from classmates and peers. It was like they wanted to say something but had no idea what to say. This also was probably exaggerated because of the state of mind I was in.

I would pass by people and I would get a tap on the shoulder, or a quick head nod as if to say, I'm thinking of you or I am praying for you." My friends would ask how I was doing and all I could say is, "I'm good, I'm ok." It's hard to pinpoint what you are really feeling when surrounded by so many people. "They wouldn't understand anyway," is what I thought. I didn't want to tell the world how I was feeling, I wanted as little attention drawn to me as possible. I had just been one of the centers of attention for nearly a week and for all the wrong reasons. I just wanted my life to be normal again, even though I was having a hard time figuring out what normal even meant.

Every time I made eye contact with people, I would start crying. I had no idea why. I would just cry for what felt like no reason. I remember going to clock in for work one time at the local grocery store, and I saw a buddy of mine and I just lost it. I couldn't even clock in because I had so much emotion still built up in me. Luckily, that day they sent me out to the garden center where there were not as many people. I was able to keep busy by organizing and watering plants. It kept me focused on something other than my situation. I was able to escape for a little while and immerse myself into task-oriented work.

To say it was difficult the first year Dad was gone would be the understatement of a lifetime. It was a struggle that I wish on no one. It was only about three weeks after my father passed that my cousin got married, and already we were asking ourselves, "Do we take a family picture?" It didn't feel right, and it felt so painful to try and smile. Luckily, my mom made the decision easy for us and said we would not be taking any family photos. It was way too soon.

Later that summer and right before my senior pictures, I found a Cardinals hat I gave my dad for Father's Day the year before. It was the first gift I gave him that I used my own money to buy. I loved baseball and to say I was a Cardinals fanatic would also be an understatement. I gave my dad his first fitted hat like the pros wear. I wanted him to be geared up for when we went to games in the future. So, when I found it, I took a sharpie and made it my way to remember him. I put his initials, age, date of birth, and date of death on that hat. It became my favorite hat, and I still have it today. He kept the hat on his nightstand and he only wore it on special occasions. It was in perfect condition. Even to this day, every time I put on that hat, I feel the good memories. They are memories of him teaching me how to play catch, grip the ball, and step with the opposite foot. I could hear the pop of the glove as I got better, and we were able to throw harder with each other as I got older. I could hear his voice in my ear, saying grip it and rip it. He never turned me down when I wanted to play. My dad and mom always knew how much I loved baseball. They would drive me to St. Louis every year at least once, if not twice to catch a game. It's a two and a half-hour drive one way to St. Louis from Jefferson City, but they knew how much I loved being at that park, watching my team play.

That hat reminds me of the goodness he had inside of him. It reminds me of the effort he gave to be a good dad and the example he gave me when we were young. It is something I carry with me to this day, now that I have my own two children. It reminds me that to be a great dad, you don't have to be perfect, you just have to be present. That's all that matters. So yes, I wear my Cardinals hat with great pride even though I live in Kansas City. The Cardinals are more than just a team to me, and baseball is more than just a game. It's where some of my best memories of my father are kept and cherished as I build new memories with my sons.

This is one of the ways sports can make a huge impact. If it is handled the right way it can create positive, long-lasting memories. I appreciate those memories so much because they helped me get through the difficult days in year one. Those days came fast and furious. All anyone would have to do is pick a holiday that first year and I promise you I had a Kleenex box attached to my hip. Even though that first year was the toughest, the years after that didn't get much easier. Birthdays, anniversaries, parties, the birth of his grandchildren and basically any celebration you could think of was and still is a reminder that he isn't here. As I observed other families together, it was now something that I used to have. It was hard accepting the fact that he wasn't going to be here to celebrate life with us. It was also a struggle to make the most of what we still had. There was a lot to be thankful for and we were very blessed by family and friends at each event we attended but showing up as a family of four was a major adjustment. It's something we eventually accepted, but I don't think we ever fully got used to it. Trying to make the unfamiliar familiar takes time, especially when it's not something you ever expected to happen and when all I could think about was how much fun it would be if he was still here.

Family photos are much easier now that our family has grown, but it still can be a challenge. I think we resist family pictures subconsciously because we still feel his missing presence. We may not even realize it or think about why we don't have very many pictures of us as a family. It still doesn't feel the same without him, and every picture feels like a puzzle missing a piece even though our family has added so many beautiful and amazing pieces. It's something I have eventually come to accept, but there are still moments when it stings knowing he is gone. It hurt when I held my first son, and I immediately thought that Dad would never hold him, and it hurt again when my second son was born because of the very same realization. He would have been an amazing grandfather, and my sons would have loved him even more than I did. I do know he is with us in spirit and I see his personality in my sons, nephew, and nieces, which is a wonderful reminder of the man he truly was.

Chapter 11: Phenomenal Family

My family filled us with so much support during our time of sudden loss and tremendous grief. My mom, sisters and I had relatives who continuously checked in with us and asked us how we were getting along. They gave us advice and empathy in times when we needed guidance and direction. My Godfather Marvin was always there to help me when I needed it, especially with house projects or car issues. My uncle Ralph was always available when I had finance questions or if I needed career advice. God filled in the gaps with what I hoped to learn from my father, and He used my family member's strengths to give me a guide on how to navigate adulthood.

Then there was my Uncle Sam. He lived close to me growing up and I would frequently ride my bike over to see him. He was the uncle that had all the fun toys. Four wheelers, tractors, heavy equipment, and anything a young boy would find fascinating since he worked for an excavation company. There was always something fun to do at his place, and he was always showing me pictures of excavation projects he was working on. He consistently made sure the four wheelers had a full tank of gas and we would ride for hours through his trails he made in the woods behind his house.

It seems like most people I talk to always have that one uncle or even a few uncles that always made things fun. I am fortunate to have many great uncles to learn from, but Sam was the uncle that made me feel like I was the son he never had. I felt like he was excited to see me every time and was constantly curious about what was going on in my life. Maybe it's because he wasn't married yet or because he lived so close, but for as long as I can remember, my Uncle Sam always made time for me.

It was him who took me out for lunch the day after Dad's suicide. He took me to one of my favorite Mexican restaurants in town and simply just tried to make me laugh. He was and still is very good at that. Still to this day, he has the most hilarious stories, especially when he talks about stories from his excavation projects. Stories that would bring tears to my eyes because I was laughing so hard. I think he saved some of the funniest ones for that day he took me to lunch. He made sure that I was going to be alright as I was going to the toughest time in my life. Mostly, I think it was because he could somewhat relate. He and my mom lost both of their parents at a very young age as well. He was about the same age I was when his father passed.

We never know how a little act of kindness sprinkled in with compassion can have an impact so deep on someone. Of all the pain and remorse I was going through, it was that lunch that helped me realize that somebody truly cared about me. More importantly a grown man, who I looked up to, made it a priority to simply spend time with me. It's those moments that all of us need during certain points in our lives. Sometimes, simply knowing that we are valued and that we matter can help us get through the most difficult of times. My sisters had similar support from other relatives as well. How blessed were we to have such a big caring family?

A couple of years later, Sam got married and shortly after that he and his wife had a baby girl. Not long after she was born, I came home from college and I got to hold her for the first time. While I was holding her, they asked me to be her godfather. I hadn't held a baby in years, not since eighth grade graduation when my cousin Gracie was born. Anna was so content when I held her. I was beyond excited to have a goddaughter. It gave me a new purpose and meaning. I realized I was going to be an example to her, and I was honored that her parents trusted me with such a significant role. Even though she was just a baby, I knew my choices mattered as she grew up. I wanted her to be excited to call me her godfather, which meant I had to make choices that would ensure she would be.

I made sure I never missed a birthday party, and as she got involved in volleyball, I made as many games as possible. I loved looking on Amazon trying to find the coolest toy when she was little and sneaking her an extra piece of cake, candy or scoop of ice cream whenever her parents weren't looking. After all, that's what my uncle did when I was growing up for me. It was my duty to return the favor or maybe, in this case, it was returning the flavor. Again, God staying faithful in finding ways for me to regain joy in my life by blessing me with my Goddaughter, Anna.

Another relative who always made time for me was my uncle Rod, who is married to my Godmother Debbie. He was my go-to uncle for all thing's sports. I was that kid who watched SportsCenter on repeat especially on days when Stuart Scott and Rich Eisen were co-hosting. In my opinion, the best duo in SportsCenter history, I'm just saying. Rod was as cool as the other side of the pillow. We could talk for hours about baseball, football, and basketball. He always had a ball ready to play catch. Well, there was one exception. The one time he had to turn me down was at his wedding when he married Debbie. I was only ten years old at the time and asked him if he wanted to go play catch as he was sitting at the head table. Even then he was thoughtful with his words and said, "Buddy, more than anything I want to go play catch and not be in this tuxedo, but I got to make sure your aunt is happy so we can play a lot more after the wedding." From my ten-year-old perspective, playing catch at their wedding seemed logical. Fortunately for me, he was true to his word and we spent many hours playing catch and shooting hoops for many years.

Rod and Debbie made me feel like the son they never had as well. I'm pretty sure Debbie was still getting me birthday gifts until I was 30. She has always had such a giving personality! I would go over to their house to watch every major sporting event. In high school, I would rather go over to their house to watch March Madness than watch it with my buddies because Uncle Rod had and still does have the big screen along with the "Jethro Bowl" of ice cream. It was always the really good ice cream too. Cookies and Cream, chocolate chip, or rocky road was always available. I never understood why the word Jethro was used, but apparently, it meant ridiculously big!

When Dad passed, I relied heavily on the examples of many of my uncles. I saw how hard they worked to provide for their families. I saw them continue to work at things in their lives to make themselves better. They were always up for a good laugh or a good joke as well, which kept me from taking life too seriously. Now I know I can always have a beer with Sam or Marvin, and Rod is always up for large bowls of ice cream. I am forever grateful for their example, and the greatest example was their commitment to their wives. I needed to see that as I grew into an adult and started thinking about what I wanted for myself.

My dad showed me how to be a great husband for 17 years. I could tell he really loved my mom. However, now that I had to move forward without him, I needed to figure out what it all meant to be a good man and a good husband. The best joke Rod still tell is, "Well Jason, I was tired of being happy, so I got married." He still throws that line out there at family gatherings and I still laugh every time he says it. Shockingly, Debbie has not found that punch line as humorous over the years, but I know Rod wouldn't have life any other way.

The continuous compassion my uncles have shown me throughout my life has helped me become who I am. The best part was that they were always there for me. There were a lot of people that told me the classic line, "Let me know if you need anything." They, however, were the few that just showed up when I needed someone the most. I'll never forget it and I will continue to pass that compassion forward to those around me. They gave me the mental release and escape I needed before and after I faced my harshest reality.

Chapter 12: Flipping the Script

U p until recently and even more so in my twenties, I would have dreams that felt as if they were real life. They felt so real that when I woke up, it took a couple of seconds for me to realize that I was just dreaming. I would wake up with intense feelings of anger, and resentment because it felt like my dad was trying to get back into my life after being gone. I got so mad during these dreams because the scenarios that played out in them felt like the ones you would see in everyday life. Looking back, it seems like these dreams could have stemmed from the suppressed emotions that I didn't want to deal with at the time. I didn't understand that feelings would eventually be expressed whether I consciously thought about them or not.

The first scenario I remember dreaming about was as if he had just left and never came back. In my dreams, he was still alive, but he drove off and decided he didn't want to be around us anymore. He was gone for years and we had moved on with our lives. Then he would come back, and I couldn't stand it. I wouldn't even talk to him and waited until he left to speak again. I felt the bitterness as I was sleeping because again it felt as if it was actually happening. It was as if he figured out that he made a regrettable decision and wanted his way back into my life. I was so hurt when he left, I didn't know how to let him back in. I thought he was just going to leave again when it was convenient for him, like he did earlier. These were all just dreams but I would wake up in a cold sweat, and I would be breathing heavier than normal. These dreams were bringing out my suppressed feelings of resentment and abandonment.

The next scenario that replayed many times was that he had left my mom and us kids for another woman and another life. This one brought on a different kind of anger and resentment. It made me more protective of my mother and sisters. All I could think about was what an asshole he was for leaving my mom for another woman. It was weird because when he was alive, that would have never happened. They had a great marriage and they were very committed to each other. It is not something he would have ever done. He was very involved with us and he loved my mom very much! This dream brought out

59

the hurt and betrayal I was feeling from his loss. Again, suppressed emotions finding ways to express themselves.

The last scenario that came up often was him being a yoyo dad. He would come around when he needed something and then he would leave. We wouldn't hear from him for months or years, and then he would show up again when he needed something. He always looked dingy and raggedy. Almost like he was homeless living out of his truck. I would yell things like, "Get out of here you dead beat!" Again, the anger and resentment in my dreams felt similar but different.

I didn't understand why these dreams were happening at the time, but now I know they were my feelings finding a way to be expressed. I hadn't gained the awareness yet of understanding how to deal with all these suppressed emotions that happen when a loved one is lost to suicide. They had been consciously pushed down and shoved aside, but when I was sleeping, they could express themselves through dreams due to me being in a more unconscious and vulnerable state of mind.

It was as if every dream I was having painted an opposite picture of who he really was. My dad was very well kept together, and he was very talented. He was very active, social, and always willing to help others. I couldn't understand the reason these dreams were implanting a picture of him that wasn't who he really was at all.

Why was I having such vivid, real dreams? Why were they festering so much anger inside of me? These were the questions

I would wake up to every time it happened. I would only have them once every couple of months, but they came regularly. It felt like I was watching a movie about my life and my relationship with my dad with multiple endings. It was as if the good memories had been held hostage because my suppressed feelings of anger, resentment, and abandonment. I had difficulty recalling all the impactful moments that were positive, like him teaching me to do things the right way, how to throw a ball, how to fish, how to drive a car, taking me to Cardinals games and all the other things he did for me. Why weren't those good memories forming my dreams?

Then it eventually registered to me that I had not healed from what had happened. I hadn't allowed myself to feel what I needed to feel in order to move forward. I didn't want to deal with the hurtful feelings, so I just ignored and dismissed them. Unfortunately, that never worked. Since I didn't embrace my pain, it surfaced in other areas. I was trying to put a lid on the feelings that didn't make me feel so great. I just wanted to laugh and be happy all the time. Feeling the hurt was something I didn't want to deal with because it was uncomfortable and quite frankly, I felt embarrassed about what happened. I didn't want people to know this about me, which meant I was allowing my outside world to be my main influence. My mom encouraged me to go to counseling, but I was stubborn and thought I could battle through it myself.

For a while, suppressing my painful feelings seemed like it worked until I would have a "dad dream." The "dad dream" was a reminder that I couldn't just ignore these feelings of pain, anger, and resentment towards him. I had to face the facts and face them head-on. I needed to look inside myself, accept my feelings and acknowledge them. It took over a decade to come to that realization, but I am thankful that I have finally gotten to that point. I finally understood this when I became a father myself. Not long after my oldest son Louis was born, while I was rocking him in his room, tears started to flow from my eyes. Thoughts of my dad never being able to hold his grandson flooded my mind and welled up my emotions. It was then I knew that I had to find a way to heal the wounds that were still there.

I had been carrying these feelings with me for over 13 years. They were limiting me in every aspect of my life. I knew I had to heal them, and I would have to start embracing them. Ironically or because of God's purpose, I was in church one day and the sermon was on forgiveness. It was God's message to me that I had to find a way to forgive my dad. I had to get to a point where I could fully forgive and let go of the feelings that were holding me back. Not only did I have to forgive him, but I had to let him know that I still loved him. I wish more than anything he was still here to play with his grandkids and be with Mom but wishing for something that isn't going to happen is wasted effort.

So, I decided to start the healing process. I got up early one morning, and whispered, "Dad, I forgive you." Crying immediately followed, but this is what was needed. I allowed myself to feel my hurts and my pains. It was so uncomfortable, and I wanted to stop, but I knew I needed to keep going. Every morning I would get up, say it a little louder and then add, "Dad, I love you." This statement also brought more tears. However, I felt myself changing in a positive way. It felt like freedom, and I could feel the joy creeping back in the depths of my soul. It felt like someone took a key and unlocked the weighted shackles of the pain I was carrying for so long. All because I decided to start the process of full and unwavering forgiveness. The more I was able to forgive him, the more I was reminded of Jesus' words in Matthew 18:21-22. When Peter asks how many times one should forgive another for wrongdoings. Jesus responded by saying forgive seventy times seven. In other words, forgive unconditionally.

This doesn't mean that I don't have boundaries or that I shouldn't stand up for myself, but what it does mean is that when I learned forgive, I took my own power back. Forgiveness helped me take back my happiness, joy, confidence and self-worth. I became aware that I deserve a life uncompromised and that is what God wants for me. When I didn't forgive my pains caused by my dad's suicide and when I was holding on to my hurt feelings, I was giving it power over me. It was detrimental to my growth and joy.

I finally reached full forgiveness on May 10, 2019. My Goddaughter Anna had just finished her 8th-grade graduation and there was a little time between the graduation ceremony and the festivities afterward. I felt my intuition telling me to go visit Dad, his headstone less than five minutes away. That is the beautiful thing about my hometown of Taos, Missouri, everything is extremely close.

I was hesitant at first, but then I was reminded that this was part of my path to forgiveness. I disregarded my resistant thoughts and I went to visit his headstone as the sun was setting. It was a beautiful sunset. The reds, oranges, and greys were picturesque. I slowly walked towards the front of his headstone and as I knelt down, I could see my reflection in the marble. I've been told many times that I look so much my father. As I knelt there I looked into my reflection, which almost made me feel as if I was talking to him. I said to him, "Dad, I hold no grudges and I am no longer angry. I wish I knew what you were going through. Maybe I could have helped and maybe you would still be here. However, I just want you to know I love you and I ask for your guidance."

I prayed that God would bring him to heaven, and I prayed that he would watch over his wife, children, and grandchildren from above. As I drove away, chills ran up my arms as my hands were on the steering wheel. They continued through my body directly to my heart. It gave me a feeling of warmth, inner peace and joy. After the graduation ceremony, I drove back to my mom's condo, and a smile naturally came across my face. Memories of the good times with my dad filled my mind and the pain was gone. My heart was full of joy again and thoughts of how I could use my God given abilities came rushing into my mind. It was during that drive home where the desire to write this book manifested in my heart and in my soul. The word "write" continued to surface in my thoughts, so that's what I did every day during the summer of 2019. It was time to stop playing small and start dreaming big.

Since Dad's passing, I have been living, I have found some transformative tidbits and pieces of wisdom that I feel are necessary to pass along to the reader. The second part of this book is about the 15 pieces of guidance that are necessary to live a life you thought you could only imagine. By consistently putting these pieces in action, you will create a life beyond anything you ever thought was possible.

Here is how you implement these pieces of guidance. Read each piece multiple times. For example, spend at least a week maybe even two focusing on one piece at a time. Then think and journal about how you can apply that one piece to your life. Finally, turn your thoughts into habits by putting these pieces into action. Within 3-6 months you will be amazed by how much you have grown and changed for the better but remember this is transformative! Transformative means it changes you for the rest of your life, not just a couple weeks or a few months.

You will find that happiness has been something inside of you this whole time. You will see that your life will continue to improve every day. The right people will come into your life exactly when you need them, and circumstances will go your way much more than ever before. You might be asking "How is this going to happen?" The answer only requires faith and then it becomes simple. However, a simple answer doesn't always mean it will be easy, especially at first. I'll even break the golden rule of teaching and give you the answer. Besides, I teach PE, all my assessments require personal action anyway. Now you may be asking yourself, "what's the answer, Jason?"

The answer is this... God's timing is always perfect, so stop messing with it by doubting or worrying. Sometimes the action you need to take requires you to do nothing but trust God's plan. Go with the flow, instead of trying to swim upstream. It's time to piece it all together and create your best life, because you matter and it's what you deserve.

Piece 1: First, You Love You

"It's not about how hard you hit. It's about how hard you can get hit and keep moving forward."
-Sylvester Stallone in Rocky

It seems as if many people in society are always looking for validation from outside sources to fill the need to belong, feel loved, cared for and to feel appreciated. We think, "If only I had the right significant other, lived in a certain house, drove that car, or went to this school, then I'd be accepted or happy." The point is that so many people ask the world to fill them up and many times the world disappoints. The reason why the world disappoints you is because it was not made to fulfill your happiness. Especially since happiness is something that you already have within yourself. You will be disappointed if you rely on other people and materialistic things to make you happy. Most material things eventually lose their luster over time and then cause you to go looking for the next new thing. I know I have fallen in that trap many times. Don't get me wrong, I think material things are great, but I want to get to a point where I don't feel like I must have them. It doesn't matter if it's a car, house, iPhone, or any other materialistic item, they are great to acquire and use, but if they're gone tomorrow it's not going to dramatically affect how I live my life.

I really like the phrase, "use things and love people." However, society encourages you to use people to get the things you want. It tells you that if you have this or that, then you will be happy. It's a completely backwards and bogus way of thinking. How many of you feel these pressures? You think you have to be in a relationship, buy a new car, buy a new house and put it all on a credit card or loan and pay it back later. Then what happens is you work so hard to get all these things and you end up still feeling lonely, empty and sad. You get bored with what you have accumulated, and you look to what's next as opposed to what's present.

Many people keep striving to have more, and they try to figure out what they can do to get more. People work long hours, become workaholics to get all the material wealth in the world, but then they lose their family in the process. Was it worth it? You can have all the money in the world, but if you have no one to share it with then are you really wealthy?

Many of us use vacations to escape life instead of using vacations to be a part of our lives. We tend to stop taking care of ourselves and eat whatever we want and then we wonder why obesity is an epidemic in our country. We can spend hours scrolling through our phones and can send a thousand messages through a screen, but can't even make eye contact and have real, engaging conversations with the people next to us.

It's time to make a change for the better. It starts by asking those around you, "Hey, how is it really going? Be honest with me." Many times, you and I don't do this because it feels uncomfortable but it's what all of us need. The great thing is you just need a few people who really care. However, there is such a disconnect being created in our society and it is leading more and more people to feel isolated. We hear about how many people feel lonely and unloved but, at the same time, many of us are unwilling to step out of our comfort zone and reach out to them.

The truth is you cannot love another person in this world until you fully love everything about you. So many of us have forgotten to love ourselves and to love who we are first.

You have to love who you are. You do this by caring about your body, mind, and soul. When you care about your body, mind and soul then your impact radiates to the world. You show others you love them by the acts of kindness you portray in your daily life. The reason why you can love others is because you've done the internal work on yourself. You can step out of your comfort zone because you know you don't need anyone's affection to fulfill you. The "all about me" attitude is needy, unsatisfying, and looking to outside sources for fulfillment but, when you say, "I am enough", you start loving yourself more. You can have everything but need nothing all at the same time. It is a bit of a paradox, but you eventually learn to love having moments when you are yourself and at the same time, understand that you are a social being at your core.

You have a right to want to feel a connection to others and feel like you belong. You can only love someone if you are comfortable with who you are, and this happens when you love yourself whole-heartedly. Do yourself a favor and be intentional about loving everything about yourself. Set a goal of working on who you are internally so you can portray it to the world externally. It's the exact opposite of society's message. Ignore society. Society tells you to live from the outside in, but what you really need to do is live from the inside out.

When you decide to live from the inside out, you will walk with a purpose and a mission. You will acquire the attitude that was created by Samuel "Golden Rule" Jones, which is what I want for myself, I want for everyone else. People will want to be around you, and you will attract connections instead of trying to force connections. You will start to realize there is an abundance of opportunities for you impact the world. You will see how you can use your resources to make a difference in the world through your mission. You will see mistakes as learning opportunities, and you will use failure as a stepping stone to figure out how to get better the next time. When you love yourself, you are fearless, but you are also conscious. You really start to think, and when you think, get emotionally involved in your ideas. Then you will realize that you can't help but act on the idea and when you act, act to impact. If you don't believe what you are doing is improving humanity, you will never be satisfied. You must love what you do and become obsessed with getting better. This is one definition of greatness. This fills your mind with desire and purpose. People will gravitate towards you when show up with energy and are excited about the day's opportunities.

Every day you have choice. You can choose to stay safe, or you can get bold and step out of your comfort zone. You can rewire how you think, and you can strive to be a little better every day. You can care about yourself a little more, you can believe in yourself and know that rejection just means there is something better on its way. Never think that you can't do something; instead, only think of how you can make your dreams come true. When you face roadblocks or when life gives you challenging circumstances, think of them as a training ground preparing you for what's next in your life. Roadblocks are not a reason to stop what you are doing. It took Thomas Edison 1000 tries to invent the light bulb and now electricity is a commonality. When a reporter asked Edison how he felt after failing 1000 times, Edison replied, "I didn't fail 1000 times. The light bulb was an invention that had 1000 steps." Thank God he didn't give up at the 999th attempt.

I overcame the tragedy of losing my father to suicide because I believed there was still an amazing life to live. That doesn't mean I never had challenging times or that I had everything figured out with the snap of a finger, but I pushed through by not giving up. I learned that I need to love myself and that learning never stops. Every day I choose to do something that will improve my life. The good news is you have that choice as well. I am learning and mastering skills that will help me pursue my dreams. Here is more good news, you also can do the same! Please be aware though, if you stop learning you start regressing, you will start feeling like many others who are unsatisfied because they stop improving themselves. They get stuck in life's routines and become hamsters on a wheel doing the same things over and over again.

Wake up in the morning, look at yourself and say, "I love you." Really mean those words and then glorify God by your actions. If you know that when you love who you are, then you can authentically love others and then you give them the freedom to love you back. It's a beautiful thing. You can go to bed every night and be proud of yourself for what you did that day. See yourself as an evolving person and you remember that you only fail when you stop trying. The world needs your story and those who criticize you are just people who wish they had the courage to do what you set out to do. Make the world a better place by giving it everything you got. A life of regrets is no life to live.

A life of "I wish I would have done this or that" just makes you feel like you are wasting your greatness. People procrastinate because they are afraid of finding out how great they can be and playing it safe is convenient and easy. They feel urges to do more, but by saying, "I'll start tomorrow" they give themselves time to stay comfortable. Then tomorrow comes and they repeat the same cycle.

What is that one thing you know you need to do, but you are procrastinating on? What is keeping you from your own greatness? If it is fear, understand that fear simply stands for Feeling Excited And Ready. Fear is just telling you to gather more information, so you are prepared. Fear is telling you that all you need is more faith.

Piece 2: Faith Over Fear

Fear is something that holds you back from your own greatness. There might be times where you have a tendency to think about everything that could go wrong as opposed to everything that could go right. I know I have thought this way on more than a few occasions, especially after the loss of my father. Thinking like this may create a reason for you stay in your perceived safe zone because you are nervous about facing your fears. For example, if you worry about looking bad or what others will think, and you end up giving your power away because of it. Fear is what causes you to doubt your abilities and it makes you timid. This is the opposite of faith and confidence. Fear and doubt will guide you to a path of mediocrity and not living up to your full potential, which is where so many people live today.

Here is what fear really is if you want to get down to the nitty-gritty: it is a mirage of scenarios that you build up in your head. As you go through life you realize more often than not you've worked yourself up for nothing. I used to do that all the time, especially when trying something I've never done before! Anytime you experience something new, fear seems to rear its ugly head. When you sense fear, you also tend to sense nervousness. Nervousness is defined as negative excitement. Fear served humanity well thousands of years ago to help us survive as a species, when we were prey and we were being potentially being hunted by predators. I would say times have changed a little since then. However, being alert can help you be aware of your current surroundings and look out for anything that might harm you. When you are cautious, you think about and analyze situations, but sometimes you can over-analyze and overthink.

You have the ability determine the risk factor by thinking through your decisions. Cautiousness can be compared to confidence because, if you are too cautious, you will never know what is possible, but if you are not cautious enough then you put yourself in situations that will elicit fear and danger. The right amount of cautiousness can help you make well-informed decisions and act on your dreams because you fully understand the risks involved. Likewise, if you have too little confidence then you feel like you are not worthy of success, or you feel like you can't learn. On the opposite side, if you have too much confidence, you don't think you need to learn anymore, and you become stagnant.

Finding the right balance of cautiousness and confidence can help you overcome any of your fears and realize that, most of the time, it is a mirage in your mind. When you experience something that initially made you afraid, you realize it wasn't that bad. You might even find enjoyment when you face and go through your fears. When confronting your fears becomes familiar, eventually you won't think twice about it. You just made the unfamiliar familiar. Think of a toddler going down a slide for the first time. For a little person, that slide looks huge, but when they face their fears and go down it, most of them love it and want to do it again and again. You and I are like the toddler going down the slide. We just have to dive in and go for it! When we realize that it wasn't that bad or it was actually fun and worth it, we will want to do it again.

Facing your fears is the most courageous act you can do, especially if you want to make a difference in the world. The world needs someone like you, who expresses boldness, courage and a willingness to overcome the things that make others nervous or scared. What if one person heard your story, and it changed their life forever? If you hide behind fear and comfort, you will never know your true impact. The world needs people who are willing to uncover their vulnerabilities because they understand something bigger is at stake. When you face your deepest, darkest fears, you give others the inspiration to face theirs as well. This is one of the reasons why I choose to write this book. To get to a point where you could say, "yes this is what I was afraid of, but I did it anyway!" Become a hero to someone. One hero can change the world. Maybe your voice was the voice that was needed for one person to speak, write, create or just simply be a better person. You never truly know how much you can impact another.

It is not an easy undertaking and, many times, speaking your truth is a delayed state of gratification. This is difficult for because we live in an "instant gratification" society. We want things now, and if it doesn't happen now or if we can't physically see it, then we think nothing is happening. What you and I fail to realize is that even though we may not be able to see it, it's happening. You reap what you sow, just like a gardener. When a gardener plants their crops they know they won't just pop up the next morning and be ready to harvest. They know it takes time and they know the crops will grow even though they can't see them. This is just like your life. What seeds are you planting in your daily life? Is fear keeping them from growing? If not, then will you be ready for the harvest? Because if you plant the right seeds, your harvest will be abundant. So much so that you can't help but share with others. Remember that your seeds will grow when you have faith. Full and unwavering faith is knowing what you want in life is coming to you. You may not know exactly when or how but believe it's coming anyway. That is the water your crops need for your life to grow. Be aware that on the other side of faith is fear and doubt. They are like your personal famine. They will dry out your dreams and stunt the growth of your faith.

Every day you have the option to choose faith or to choose fear. There is only room for one in your thoughts, words, and actions. They do not live in harmony with each other. Choosing fear is safe and will get you exactly what you already have. Nothing more and nothing less, just more of the same. By choosing faith, you will start to live the life you have always wanted. On top of that, your actions, words, and thoughts will push you through fear to a place you never thought was possible. Faith will lead you to an abundance of joy, and happiness. It will also give you the energy to fuel your effort.

I recently chose to live a faithful life. I lived for too long in my comfort zone. I wanted to be safe because of my dad's suicide. I had so much fear that something bad was going to happen and I limited myself because of it. I tried to avoid uncomfortable situations many times because of the fear of feeling similar pain. I have now realized that what controls your destiny is your thoughts. I learned this by reading books like *Think and Grow Rich* by Napoleon Hill, *Code of the Extraordinary Mind* by Vishen Lakhiani, and Bob Proctor's series on Wallace Wattles's book *The Science of Getting Rich*. I know now my thoughts create my reality and I am growing in my faith. I know what I want in life is coming to me as I reach toward my goals. Any time a doubt tries to sneak in I reject it and immediately start thanking God for everything I have. It is through my faith that I have written this book. I believe that I can make an impact by reversing mental illness and be an activist for suicide prevention. Unwavering faith plus daily gratitude are two essential pieces that I used to put my life back together.

Piece 3: Gratitude

Gratitude is the art of appreciation and the foundation of prayer. The best thing that you can blend with faith is gratitude. Every day, I either write in my journal or I sit in silent gratitude. I start off by saying, "I am so joyous and thankful for another opportunity to live my life today." Then I will say, "I am so joyous and thankful for my wife, kids, and my health." I say seven to ten things I am thankful for. I love starting off my day and ending my day with this gratitude exercise because it reminds me of how good my life really is. Even though I have endured a great loss, I have gained so much since the passing of my dad in the spring of 2003. Gratitude helps me focus on my gains, my wins, and all the good that continues to happen in my life. I am even thankful for the things that I wanted at one time but didn't get. It helped me realize that I probably wouldn't want some of those things now that I thought I wanted at the time. By applying gratitude, my life keeps improving. The great thing about gratitude is that it is a free to express. Anyone can choose to be thankful and it's up to you to make that choice for yourself. When you display gratitude and appreciation, you are not only showing it to the people around you, but you are also showing it to God. You stay connected to God's presence in your life by seeing the good He is bringing you. Showing gratitude opens your awareness to what's going on in your life. Eventually, you learn to appreciate even the smallest things, like a hug, a beautiful sunset, or even a small act of kindness. Whatever you're thankful for, gratitude is a skill that needs to be constantly practiced and it is worth repeating. When you say thank you and when you mean thank you with all your heart, you become something more than what you ever thought was possible. There is something inside of you that desires to be more because you know the good you can do. Suddenly you become extremely thankful for every opportunity because every opportunity is training you for your next big thing.

Gratitude is the key that opens the doors to new possibilities and gives you the right opportunity at the right time. It will get you to where you want to go with constant practice and with an emotional attachment. You must connect your heart to your words, or your words will simply be empty thoughts. It is your heart and your feelings that launch you into action because of your sincere gratitude. By practicing gratitude, you will get to a point where you understand that by not acting, you are doing a disservice to the world. Eventually, with great intent and consistent practice, gratitude will simply be a part of who you are. You know it, you feel it, and then you live it. Even the things you might not understand, you are thankful for because you know eventually there will be a purpose.

I choose to be thankful regardless of my circumstances. I was thankful for the support around me as I pushed through the times that were bleak and blurry. When I wasn't sure what to do next, I am thankful that God was always there giving me guidance, even when I didn't realize it. Hindsight is always 20/20 and I can say "I should have" or "I could have" done this, but everything in my life has happened for a reason. So, I choose gratitude and I look for the lesson God is teaching me.

I wish every day my dad was here with us. I would have loved to create more lasting memories with him. I wish he could have experienced holding, teaching and playing with his grandchildren, because he would have been a damn good grandpa. Unfortunately, he made a choice that I know he really didn't want to make. His suicide was a wakeup call for me. It has taught me that I have to take care of not just my body but my mind and my soul as well. I have to be aware of the thoughts that I'm thinking and consciously place gratitude in my life to spark positivity and feel connected to what I have been given.

I know that every day I have a choice to make, regardless of what I feel like doing. I make it simple and I choose gratitude. I choose to mix my gratitude with faith because when I add faith and gratitude together it equals positive, clear, and concise thoughts. Positive thoughts turn into desires that I get emotionally involved in and I launch myself back into my work to impact as many people as possible. I can't help but take action because of my faith and gratitude.

Those two elements are an unstoppable partnership and a force that will make anyone limitless with consistent practice. I can't help but repeat that faith and gratitude are available for anyone who chooses them, regardless of your current situation or circumstance. Keep your faith, practice gratitude and watch your world change around you. An amazing life is right around the corner by taking that first step towards gratitude and faith. When you walk towards faith and gratitude, they will walk closer to you as well.

Regardless of what you do, you must prepare yourself to follow through with your plans by using faith and gratitude. Dismiss doubt and fear immediately when they try to make their way into your mind. Let them know they have no place in your mind and they are not welcome. Keep the vacancy in your mind, reserved for faith and gratitude and your actions will be plentiful and highly impactful.

Piece 4: Comfortable with Uncomfortable

Every time Lebron James goes to a workout or a training session, he is not satisfied until he has gotten out of his comfort zone. He tells his trainers if he isn't uncomfortable then they are not doing their jobs. This is how he made it to the mountain top. He knows that being uncomfortable is a sign of growth. He understands that in order to get what you want, you have to give something in return. There are very few things in life worth having that you do not have to give something for. LeBron has the willingness to continuously go beyond his talents and abilities. He stretches himself a little more, so he can become more. He keeps working and growing. It gets easier, but the work itself isn't necessarily easy. It's the challenge that pushes him to new heights.

This is a great lesson for those of us that want something more in our life. You and I have the capability to be more, do more and have more. The choice is always yours and only yours. You can choose to push yourself and be comfortable with uneasiness. You can look at your mess-ups and mistakes as opportunities for growth and skill acquisition. You also can choose to stay with what you have always known, which is what many people do. It doesn't matter what your passion is, you will need to push past your comfort zone if you want to do more, be more, and have more.

Life is actually very simple, but our media and society like to make things seem more complicated. We make it more complex when we let what the outside world control how we think. I suggest you flip that around and keep a resilient mindset by filtering your thoughts and rejecting negative messages. Then you can choose to act and follow your passion. You can rise up, be determined to make an impact and choose to improve yourself both internally and externally in order to become the best version of yourself. You deserve that, and your family and friends deserve the best version of you as well. The only regrets you will have in life are the opportunities you didn't take. You will regret not going for what you really wanted and settling for average. What you won't regret is going after something bigger than yourself to make the world a better place.

I choose to tackle mental illness. Each of us need healthy minds to think clearly, create ideas, and lift our emotions. When you have a healthy mind, your body naturally responds, and you make better decisions about being active and feeling positive about the situations you face in life. You start to know that no matter what, something better is coming, regardless of what life throws your way. That's when you begin to build self-confidence and you start to believe that you can achieve practically anything. When you have a healthy mind, you build a healthy heart that is compassionate and empathetic towards others. You are able to see other people's perspectives and have a greater understanding of where they are coming from. It doesn't mean you have to agree, but at least you can relate and be understanding. Finally, when you have a healthy mind, you can trust your soul, which is your conscious voice guiding you and giving you hunches on decisions you know you need to make. Your intuition is almost always right, especially when you learn to trust it. It also provides insight when you don't know where to turn, or what to do. You may be asked to do things that are uncomfortable or that don't make sense but when uncomfortable becomes your comfortable you recognize it immediately and realize that what is on the other end of uncomfortable is absolutely worth it.

Here is how you get to where you want to go. First, you start with your mind, then you have to connect your mind to your heart. Thoughts must be created and then they must be felt. A feeling with thought is an idea that makes its mark on humanity and creates a better world for everyone. You have a mind that is powerful and divine. In fact, because it is so powerful, there are many times you are unaware of how influential you truly are. You might be unaware because, if you're like me, you were never really taught how to use your mind. Do you know that you can choose to think anything you want to think? Did you also know you can reject anything that goes against what you want for yourself? You don't have to allow the naysayers or critics to beat you down. You just need to continue to imagine, create and take action.

You take action by using your will, which helps develop self-discipline. Your will uses intuition to guide you on what to do. Then it is your job to take action on your passion. This will push you into uncomfortable situations, and that is a good thing! The reason it's a good thing is because that's where growth happens. If you keep your focus and you use your will, then your accomplishments will follow. These accomplishments are possible because you choose to think first and those thoughts turn into more than a passion, they become your obsession. The thoughts you have can fuel your emotions and direct your actions. This is when you look at your accomplishments and celebrate them. You celebrate them and subsequently start the process over again, then you figure out how you can make it better.

You are always moving in a direction; it is up to you to determine which way you are taking yourself. If you choose to stay safe and stay in your comfort zone, you will slowly wither like a flower that's getting just enough water to survive.

However, if you choose to go beyond what you have done in order to grow and advance, you will make a profound impact on not only yourself but those around you as well. Again, it always goes back to the choices you make. You can choose to live your dreams by doing the thing that scares you the most, because the life you want is on the other side of that discomfort.

All you need to do is remember to use your God-given free will when you need a kick in the butt or a restart. If you demand excellence from yourself, then others won't have to ask you for it. When you want it so bad that you can't help but act, that's when you know you've found what you desire. When you procrastinate and worry about what others will think, you are not only hurting yourself, but you are also hurting humanity because what you have to give is worth so much more than what you chose to keep inside. If you can make a positive impact on just one person, then you have succeeded. You succeeded because you choose to be uncomfortable and maybe that's what that one person needed to see. You never know, you might be the difference that gets someone out of their funk and into their greatness.

Piece 5: Self-Discipline Over Self-Distraction

Today's world continues to advance quicker every day as technology continues to improve. It is truly amazing what we have been able to accomplish over the last 100 years and even more so over the last ten years. We can access the world's information on a tiny screen and learn about anything we want at the touch of a button. We have apps that make life so convenient that we don't need to leave our house if we don't want to. Just when we think, "How can they possibly add something more to what is already here?" a new update comes out that seemingly makes life even more convenient. We live in a world of abundance. It is truly a great time to be alive. Whether it be a social injustice or a magnificent breakthrough, we can let our voices be heard. Social media has created more transparency in our world in nearly every aspect of life.

However, it can be difficult sifting through how to know what is accurate and what is just someone's opinion. This is where you have to trust your intuition and where you can choose your thoughts. If something doesn't sound accurate, you can fact check it to find more accurate information. More than ever you need to have the ability to think your own thoughts and reject thoughts that are contrary to your success.

It can be easy to get lost in the social media world and be digitally distracted as Robin Sharma points out. As great as technology is, if you do not practice discipline when using technology, you can become distracted, and it can disrupt your ability to think. You might read posts that stir emotions because you allow what other people post to influence you. It is very easy to waste away hours thumbing through general information that leaves you feeling worse than you did before.

I admit that I am currently rewiring myself to get out of being so digitally distracted. I would spend at least an hour or two a day just looking at social media and more times than not I would ask myself, "What the heck am I doing?" I've wasted too many hours of my life reading people's rant about how sucky their life is and I wasn't realizing the effect it was having on me. I read people complain about things that really didn't affect their day to day life. Then there is the other side of the social media spectrum where everyone has their highlight reel. Their lives all seem to be perfect, and I realized I was comparing myself to others highlights. It was making me feel like my life wasn't as good as theirs, and it was the biggest lie I could tell myself. I was allowing these feelings of inferiority to come into my life and it was causing me to doubt my own abilities.

I think the main reason that I was so digitally distracted was because it helped me escape from some of my experiences. As I looked at other people's posts, I was playing the victim game. All I could think about was how good everyone else's life looked. At some point I realized that enough was enough. I decided that instead of comparing myself to others, I would be excited for them. I would react to a post with a heart or a smile and be genuinely happy that they got to experience a certain event or vacation. I told myself, "I know my time is coming as well, I just have to be patient." I love to create win-win situations in life. I remind myself that what I want for my life is also what I want for others. It helps me keep things in perspective.

One year during Lent, I decided to give up social media and see how I felt by not being so distracted. Within a week, I felt happier and more confident. I was more focused on what was going on in my life and I was way more productive. Things that used to take me 30 minutes took about 15 and I just felt better about myself.

I concluded that I can choose to be focused and disciplined, or I can choose to be distracted. If I choose to be focused and disciplined, it might require me to make uncomfortable changes and do things that are going to push me out of my limits. However, if I choose to be distracted then I could put life on cruise control and just be average. I decided I wanted something more in my life and that I wanted to be more than average. I would continually hear my consciousness tell me that I am made for greatness and that I am meant to do more with my life than look at funny cat videos or watch Dude Perfect perform crazy stunts on YouTube. I am not saying that these are bad things, because I love a good video just like the next person. However, I gained an awareness that even though entertainment is fun and necessary at times, being engaged in something I am passionate about is going to lead me to a more fulfilling life.

I used to feel like I was wasting my time and my life by continuously searching for something to entertain me. When I realized I had a hard time just sitting in silence and felt the urge to pick up my phone to look busy, I knew I needed to change my habits. I was not ok with myself and my life, and I was choosing to be distracted instead. I could only hide behind distraction for so long and ignoring my life's challenges wasn't going to make them go away. They were still there looking for me to find solutions for them.

By choosing discipline, I am changing my life for the better. I deserve the best that life can give me, and discipline is the vehicle that will get me where I desire to be. Discipline is what will bring me the life I only thought was possible in my dreams. Discipline is what throws me into action; it helps me stay focused to impact my world internally and externally. It is what helps me find my purpose and gives me the energy to go beyond my comfort zone. There are times where I don't like discipline, but I always like the results that come with choosing discipline. Every day, I give myself commands to follow, because I know those commands will bring a life full of abundance. I can't say I'm always perfect, but every time I don't do something I said I was going to, I feel the lie and I don't like lying to myself.

It doesn't matter what other people think and say. Remember, all that matters is choosing to be your best, so you can do your best and that will give you the best in return. You have everything you need and when you know that you are enough by simply just being who you are, discipline becomes easier. It becomes easier because you don't feel like you need to prove yourself to anyone. You only need to prove it to yourself.

You start casting out fears of judgment in order to fulfill your mission and to live your purpose. Authenticity is also manifested through discipline because it requires you to grow and learn about who you really are. When you learn to discipline yourself, you don't need others to discipline you. You know what you need to do, and you do it. It sounds so simple, yet many of us make it so complicated because we choose distraction and we choose to live life on the surface because it's easier.

However, no one changed the world by staying on the surface or standing idly on the sideline. I challenge you to choose discipline over distraction and then observe the beautiful changes it brings to your life. You will get to the point where you feel like if you don't act, you are only delaying your impact and delaying your impact could be the difference in the lives of those close to you. The world needs your words, and it needs your message to give others hope who are in despair. It lets others see that what you made possible is also possible for them. It could be a family member, a neighbor, a friend, or in front of an auditorium full of people you have never met! It doesn't matter if it is one person or 1000 people. Give everyone the impression that they matter and that they are valued. How can you leave an impactful impression on all those you encounter daily?

I want you to know that just because a tragedy may creep unexpectedly into your life, it doesn't have to define who you are, and it doesn't have to break you. It may bend you, twist you, flip you upside down, and gut-punch you but you always have a choice. I challenge you, if confronted with a hardship, to come back stronger, wiser and with more resilience. Bring a force so impactful that you help others see God's beauty and glory through the faith you show, even when the light is dim. Keep pushing yourself through it because discipline told you to keep going and have faith that something much better is coming.

Piece 6: Expression Over Suppression

When did being a man get associated with never expressing feelings? It is ingrained so deep in our society that men showing emotions, especially sadness or pain, is somehow viewed as a form of weakness. I hear boys get told to "Suck it up!" and "Stop crying!" all the time. What's wrong with a cry occasionally? It can be a good and healthy thing. There is a time and a place where crying can help the grieving process, and help you work through physical or emotional pain. You become more in tune with your body when you can be free to express how you are feeling. When you are free to express how you feel, you become stronger and more compassionate. You were given these emotions for a reason and when they are expressed in a healthy way, you can gain a higher level of self-awareness and show empathy towards others.

I think there is a legitimate reason kids tend to cry more often at certain times. It is because everything is new to them and it can get overwhelming quickly. They are learning what it is like to be human. If you look at life from their perspective, they are always going through something that is unfamiliar. Every day they are experiencing things they have never seen or felt before. Adults have been through struggles, heartbreak, and tragedy. They tend to brush off things that their kids get upset with and think they are no big deal. On the other hand, from the child's perspective, it is a big deal. They don't comprehend the difference because they have less experience. When their toy gets taken from them for the first time, it's a big deal! Things like their first day of school, or their first sleepover at a friend's house, are all big deals and they may become a little nervous and clingy. You can become more relatable by trying to see their perspective and think about what they might be going through. The same goes for those who experience the loss of a loved one.

Unfortunately, there are many adults/teenagers that never learn how to truly handle painful events. Maybe you are one of them, I certainly was. Many of us, including myself, suppress feelings of pain because they are not enjoyable. It hurts and we would rather just not deal with it, but the truth is people end up hurting themselves even more by suppressing their feelings instead of expressing them.

Emotions that go suppressed will eventually surface one way or another. It's like a bucket getting filled up with water; if the bucket isn't emptied, eventually the water will overflow. I also like to use the example of soda in a bottle. When you keep the soda bottle still and gently twist the cap, the pressure is released easily. There may be a few bubbles, but everything stays in the bottle and it is easy to drink. On the other hand, when a soda bottle has been shaken or dropped pressure builds inside the bottle. If you open the cap right away soda flies everywhere. This is like your feelings and emotions. Expressing them to people you trust a little bit at a time will help you first recognize your emotions then feel, express, and release them in a healthy way. When you suppress emotions, you are essentially shaking your own soda bottle. The cap will get twisted off eventually and your emotions will get the best of you. You will say things you don't mean, and act in a way that is not who you truly are.

Your emotions and feelings will surface at some point no matter if you suppress them or express them. However, there is a big difference in how they are displayed if you can learn to be expressive. A great way to express feelings to others you trust is using "I feel" statements. This is when you can recognize that there is an emotion inside of you and expressing this emotion will give you validation that you were heard. That's what you really want anyway. You want to be heard, and you want validation. Validating your feelings doesn't mean that you think you are always right, but what it does mean is that you feel cared about. Here is an example of what I mean. Sometimes, I have what my wife would call a "frown face." She has said to me, "I feel like you're mad at me when you have that frown on your face." The fact is I'm not mad at her at all. Most of the time, I am just thinking, but through my facial expressions I gave off the indication that I was upset about something. My wife's ability to express how she felt helped us communicate, and therefore, I now try to be more aware of my facial expressions.

I really could have used the "I feel" strategy after my dad's passing. I truly never knew how to express the hurt, pain, anger, abandonment, and resentment I was feeling. I had suppressed it for so long and eventually, these feelings surfaced as personal insecurities, indecisiveness, immaturity and/or apathy. I would repeatedly ask myself questions lie, "Will people like me?" or "Will I be able to make friends?" I would overthink almost every decision, especially if I found myself attracted to a woman. I used to get so nervous and if I reached out to a girl and she didn't respond, I always thought there was something wrong with me. I didn't have the confidence I needed to be ok with being me, because I never allowed myself to fully feel and then heal the wounds that my father's suicide left.

It wasn't until a friend of mine convinced me to go on a retreat in college and I was introduced to the power of journaling. It was a retreat called Awakening. It was during that retreat that I heard other college kids talk about the things they had gone through, and it made me feel like I wasn't alone. It helped me relate to others that had things they needed to work on as well. After every presentation, I got a chance to journal and reflect. I let everything out through writing. There might have been smoke rolling off the pen as I continued to write with such ferocity. It was a release that I had never felt before. It was like more weight was being lifted off my shoulders. It had been close to five years since I lost my dad. You can imagine how much emotion one could build up over those five years. What I loved about journaling was I could release my emotions at any time, and I could do it when I was by myself. Some days I would write more than others, but it was and still is a tool I use to help keep my mind and body calm. It helps me release any repressed feelings and I can think and act with more clarity. The point is there are multiple, healthy ways to express emotions. Find one that works for you! If you don't like talking to people, try journaling. You will be amazed at how much better you feel and how much better life gets when you learn how to express what you are feelings as opposed to suppressing them.

Piece 7: Empathy Instead of Sympathy

The last thing I needed after my dad's passing was everyone's sympathy. I know everyone had good intentions when they offered their deepest sympathies but feeling sorry for me and my family wasn't going to make life better. It wasn't going to change the difficulties we were about to face. The definition of sympathy is feeling pity or sorrow for one's misfortunes. The last thing I needed was someone to pity me as well. Also, I feel like most of us use sympathetic phrases as a cop-out. I understand that we can't help but feel sorry for people who are experiencing tragedy and many times, it's hard to even know what to say to people. We live in a society where everyone wants everybody to feel like butterflies and roses every day. We are always trying to cheer people up. Again, these are great intentions, but if we don't allow people to feel the pain of their situation, they will never know the power they have in the future to change others' lives because they learned how to cope with their misfortunes.

Pain can be a great teacher if you are willing to learn from it. Is it going to be enjoyable? I would say probably not, at least hasn't been for me. However, it may be what is necessary for growth and to find purpose. There is always a lesson to be learned from every circumstance. Once you've learned that lesson, improving your life get easier. You can make something of yourself because you've experienced the depths of your life's valley and can now climb the mountain. Lace up your boots, get your mind right, and take life one step at a time.

Sympathy doesn't really offer that. Sympathy says just wallow in your pain, feel bad for yourself, play the victim, play the "woe is me" card and then you have an excuse to act any way you want. In many ways, sympathy is right. You can act and do whatever you want, but what you are not free from is the consequences of your actions. Maybe it's something you have never thought about before and have gotten burned in life because you thought that there would be no repercussions for your actions. There is always a reaction to every action.

Sympathy invites excuses because you feel like you have been wronged in life, but the problem is victims never win and people will only feel bad for you for so long. If you wake up in the morning with air in your lungs and you can breathe, then you have a duty to make the world a better place. Every day you don't do that, then you are wasting the talents and abilities given to you by God Himself.

This is why I choose empathy instead of sympathy. When I show someone empathy, they know I care too much about them to let them sit and sulk in their misfortunes. I tell them to get up and step forward, and it doesn't matter if you're not sure which way to step. Just get up and keep pushing. Life does get better over time. I don't have to completely understand their pain, but what I need to do is encourage them to feel it, then fully forgive and have the faith that it will get better. My story is living proof that you can climb out of any difficult situation and still reach the top of the mountain. If you continue to look ahead and think, "What good is going to come from this?" and you believe something better coming then that is when you have acquired full faith. This is a skill that takes practice just like any other skill. Life can seem very gloomy at times, but if you choose to focus your thoughts on your life constantly improving, then that is what will happen.

Two men came into my life right when I needed them, and their example of empathy is something I still cherish today. Jeff and Tim were Young Life leaders from Mizzou. Their mission was to show high school kids they cared, and that life can be so fulfilling. I needed good influences to look up to more than ever. I was in a very vulnerable place and could have followed any path. The loss of my father hit me hard and gave me feelings of abandonment, unworthiness, and the need for someone to notice me. Luckily, they were there for me and I am forever grateful for the example that they set. They showed me how to treat others by being compassionate, kind, fun, tough and most importantly be proud of who I am. They showed me how to handle myself when things didn't go my way, and how to respond when I face criticism from others. To this day, I still value their example. I see how they love their wives and kids and how they present themselves professionally. I take note of how they not only show up but show up prepared and dedicated regardless of what they are doing. They live with passion and purpose. There is a calming zeal and aura about them where they can be enthusiastic but at the same time be so poised. They never allow their emotions to control their decisions, and they live to impact others.

The most important thing I learned from them is how to be a helper. They told me to always try to find ways to help others. Never be afraid to lend a hand to those in need and speak up. Tell people what they need to hear, not necessarily what they want to hear. That is what Tim and Jeff did for me. They were always honest with me and gave me advice. They would ask me questions so I would check myself and make sure I was making good decisions. That is empathy and that is why empathy is so much more powerful than sympathy. Empathy demonstrates to people that you care, sympathy just tells people that you care.

There is so much truth in the statement "actions speak louder than words".

When you show others empathy, sometimes no words are needed. Just lending a shoulder to cry on, giving a hug, or calling a friend just to check in could mean everything to someone. The real power in connecting with others is empathy. It is the glue that holds humanity together.

Now, you can learn something but until you put it into practice, it's just something you know. Empathy is no different. It took me a while to grasp this concept. I was always nervous about telling people what I was really thinking because I didn't want to go through something like what I just went through with my dad. I didn't want to lose good friends or people who showed interest in me. However, I've realized that empathy makes me relatable, and approachable. Empathy allows me to feel what others are feeling and gives a deeper sense of understanding of what others might be dealing with. I am more patient with others and a better listener because I started implementing empathy in my life. Try it for yourself and see the changes it makes in your life.

Piece 8: Presence Over Presents

Attention is a basic need that all humans desire to some degree. As adults, a little acknowledgement goes a long way, especially when we feel like we have put a lot of time and effort into something. The need for attention is even more evident in young children. They will do anything to meet the need to be noticed. Children want to know that their parents care about them and their interests. They want to know that they are seen and heard. They want to feel connected to those they are around the most, and attention gives them that connection. If they feel something is taking that attention away from them, they will do almost anything to get it back. Whether what the child is doing is perceived as good or bad, to the child they are getting attention and that is considered a win for them.

They take notice of the things that get them attention. A few examples are when they look right at you, turn their cup over and spill water everywhere or when they dump all their toys out with no intention of playing with them. At least that's what my three-year-old does. It is their way of communicating that their needs are currently not being met.

What children are really wanting is someone to interact and be present with them. Maybe they are spilling water on the floor because they feel like we haven't spent enough time with them that day. We have to remember that we are setting an example for our children. Staying present with our children is a very simple request but many times it gets complicated because we live in a world where it is easy to be distracted by technology.

I was at a park about a month ago, running around with my toddler son, and I saw parents everywhere disengaged with their children because they had their noses in their phones. Parents were isolating themselves and their children from personal engagement and relationship building because a video, Facebook post, or email was more important. How silly does that sound? Yet, I see it all the time and you probably do as well.

I've been guilty of it myself, but one day when I was journaling, I wrote down that I wanted to be the best father possible. Then the idea came to me that I can't be distracted and great at the same time. I had to put my phone down, turn off the screens and give my sons and my wife the attention they deserve. I needed to be both physically present and consciously engaged with my family and others. I am still working on getting better and I still need reminders occasionally. Old habits die hard, but when I think about what's most fulfilling in life, I am quickly made aware that life is about making memories and creating unforgettable moments. Do I want my kids to remember that Daddy was always distracted as they grew up? I would rather them remember that I lived a balanced life and stayed present when I was with them.

The best news in all of this is that being a great parent doesn't mean you have to have it all figured out or that you have to be perfect. If you just show that you care, most of the time that is all your kids are asking for. They may ask for it in different ways but at the end of the day they just want to know their mom or dad cares about what happens to them. They want to know that they are enough. The best thing you can tell your children is that regardless of what they do, you will love them.

You won't like every decision they make, and you won't understand them at times either, but if your kids know they can come to you when they mess up, that is a game-changer. Here is a question to always ask yourself, "How have I gotten better as a father or a mother today?" What have you studied about childhood behaviors that may help you understand why they are doing what they are doing? I recommend checking out the work of Shelly Lefkoe or Rhea Lalla, who are two masterminds of modern parenting. Maybe your children are acting in a certain way because they know how to get your attention.

Underestimating their intelligence is always a mistake. They know more, feel more, and understand more than we realize.

Unfortunately, there are some people that would rather just buy their children stuff than spend time with them. They think that having the latest gadgets and toys will keep their children happy. However, material things were not meant to replace human connection. Today, we are more connected to the outside world than ever through our devices and the internet, but many of us still feel disconnected from our family, friends, co-workers and people in general. We have to regain our ability to connect with each other. It can help ease those moments when we feel alone and/or down on our luck.

Be present with your families, children, and the people you come in contact with. Some of the best things you can give people are authenticity, compassion, and empathy. When people feel like you care about them, you can change someone's world and that is how the world gets changed. Nothing will ever replace feeling cared about by another human.

Nothing can replace a human's ability to show kindness and compassion. Those are also game-changers in today's world. I don't care how advanced technology gets, the human connection will be the only thing that can meet your most basic needs beyond food and shelter. It used to be a lot easier to spot kindness and compassion because there wasn't as much to distract you. All you had was other people and how you spent your time was connecting with those around you. Relationships seemed to be more meaningful because you couldn't hide behind a screen and make yourself look busy. Let's be honest for a moment, most of the time what you are looking at on your phone is not that important. It's time to get back to making your presence felt by being contagious in a positive way. Exuding positive vibes and giving out positive energy can make an amazing difference in your life and those you around you.

While the masses are stuck in their devices, try to be the one that brings them out of their digital hypnosis. Help others realize there is more to life. Show people how to really live by being an example of what to do to live out your inner greatness. This could be the catalyst that reverses the mental illness epidemic that is negatively impacting our society, and it will give you a sense of purpose to give your best to those around you. You can become more aware of your actions and ask yourself, "Why am I doing what I'm doing?" Everything starts with how you think, and if you think of others and how you can become more connected to each other, it will be a cure that you may have never seen before. You can nurture yourself by choosing thoughts wisely and by choosing to be present with others through their celebrations and their tribulations.

Forget the presents and just be present. Create memories through experiences and meaningful conversations. There is no possession that can completely fulfill you. Every day you have a chance to create unforgettable moments through the human experience, but it is up to you to make those moments happen.

Ask yourself how you want to remember your life and what you want others to remember about you. Always be thinking about the legacy you want to leave behind. What would people say about you right now? Because it is possible that right now you might have the legacy of addicted to devices. Is that how we want to be remembered? It's a hard question, but a necessary question. How would your life change if you asked yourself daily what you want to be known for? Would you start changing some of your actions?

Piece 9: Action Over Work

There is something about the word "work" that seems to have a negative connotation. Maybe it is because so many people feel dissatisfied when they are working at their jobs. Many people complain about Monday because there is a full work week ahead and they dread what they do. Instead of seeing their situation as an opportunity, they see it as an obligation. There is a common misconception that in order to make a lot of money, you have to work long hours and even weekends on occasion. You feel like you have to trade your time for money. When you work just to earn a paycheck, it will leave you feeling unsatisfied with how you are living your life.

Many of us crave comfort in our job. The thought of leaving our comfort zone at the job we have been doing for years gives a us so much anxiety that we just stay because we feel secure and safe. You might have experienced this yourself, or you currently feel this way. You tend to get caught up in the thought that you will be safe and secure in your job even though you might be dissatisfied. Then when you come home every night you justify staying in a job you dislike because "at least you have a job". This could be keeping you from pursuing your passion and finding a way to create a better world for yourself. You can settle and stay in your routine because it's safe and you will pretty much know what your day will be like. Honestly, there is nothing wrong with that. However, do you find yourself quick to complain about never having enough income, not enjoying your coworkers, or not enjoying the job itself? If you aren't willing to take a chance on something else, then there is no reason to complain. You will find that going after your dreams and passions is more fulfilling. It might take some time to establish yourself, but wouldn't you rather take action on something you love than work on something you hate?

Here is how taking action is different than working. When you take action, it is something you are choosing to do. There is a passion and a mission behind why you are doing what you are doing. Somehow your life has been affected and you decided that there is something inside of you that you can give to the world. There is something you can contribute that will give you the satisfaction of making a difference. It may require you to get out of your comfort zone and require you to develop new skills, but at least you will feel fulfilled.

Even though I have never written a book before, but I decided that I was doing more harm than good by not telling my story and by not writing. I decided to dive in, and I would figure out how I could write the best book possible to impact as many lives as possible. I made the decision to act and write this book because of how my dad's suicide deeply affected my life, and how I never want anyone to experience what I went through. I stopped making excuses on why I didn't think it was possible and only started thinking about how I could make it possible. I realized I had a story that could change the world and that by writing a book I could impact and inspire millions. I finally got to a point where I understood that people needed someone to relate to them, and God was asking me to have the courage to fight the darkness with light.

I gave myself commands like "write a thousand words a day" and "reread what you have already typed to see if it can sound better or if there are any grammar errors." I typed with tears rolling down my face because of the emotions that stirred as I relived the moment when I lost my dad, but I did it because the world needs to know that valuing your mind and your life is one of the best things you can do for yourself. I felt like fathers needed to know that the best thing they can give their kids is their love and presence. If only my dad knew that no job was ever worth his life and that we would figure it out. If he only

113

knew that I would rather have him quit his job than quit his life, maybe my story would not be a narrative at all, and he would still be here with us.

If you are a father, I challenge you to always think of your family and know that they are always better off with you than without you, especially your children. Always have the mindset that things will continue to improve in your life. If you hate your job and it starts to overtake your mind, then start finding ways to blaze your own trail, pursue a passion and look at tough times as training lessons for what's next. You must value your life, so your children learn to value theirs. Take care of yourself first, so you can have the energy needed to be a great spouse/companion and a great parent.

I challenge you to take action and think of only best-case scenarios. Then think about the feeling you get when those thoughts come true. These are the feelings you need so you can't help but to act. When you feel the excitement and the joy it spurs you into action. Regardless if it is being a better person, parent or professional, choosing and then feeling your thoughts are critical to your success. You may know what to do in your head, but if you don't feel it in your heart then your thoughts are just illusions.

Stay in the present moment and ask yourself if what you are doing right now is leading you to a better future. Remember, you can be in continuous prayer by taking action. What do the words' "action" and "impact" have in common? Well, by taking

ACTion you manifest impACT in other people's lives. It is not a coincidence that the word act is in both of those words. Every act you take creates an impact on yourself and those around you. You can create a positive or negative impact based on the actions you choose to take. What impact are you currently making with your actions? Are you changing your life for the better? I can tell a lot about a person very quickly by watching how they act, and they can probably do the same by watching me. It's almost like you can pinpoint exactly what others are thinking based on the actions they take. It's because your thoughts and your actions are so closely aligned. Act to impact and notice how you feel after you realize that you are the difference.

Piece 10: Prayer: A Balance of Moving Feet and Folded Hands

Prayer is more than just going to church once a week; it is something that should be interwoven in every fiber of your existence. From when you wake up to when you go to bed, everything you do is a reflection of your prayer life and who you are. It doesn't matter what you say you are going to do until you actually go out and do it. You can fold your hands and pray for the things you need but if you don't move your feet then why should God answer? The Bible says ask and you shall receive, but you have to be willing and ready to receive what you ask for through your actions and your words. Also, are you willing to have patience? Everything happens in God's time, which might be different than your time.

God will give you everything you need at the right time and He will give you everything you want based on your purpose. Why do you want a lot of money? Are you going to help others with it? Why do you want a big house? Are you going to host and serve others? Regardless of your wants, you need to always be checking your motives for why you desire the things you want in life. In and of themselves, things are not good or bad. It's how you choose to use the things you are asking for that will bring you fulfillment or leave you feeling empty. It doesn't matter how much money is in your bank account, or the size of your house if your motives don't give you the desire to help others.

God is all-knowing and He is omnipresent. He will be your eternal guide if you listen, observe, and act when He tells you to move your feet. Faith without works is dead, plain and simple. Don't believe me? Go ahead, put this book down and read James 2:14-26. Memorize this scripture and have it become a part of who you are. Your life will be full of abundance and joy. The desire and understanding of what you need to do will launch you into action and your life will be more than you ever thought it could be.

Through praying with your feet, you can get to a point in your life where you can have anything you want, but never need any of it. You become much more than the things you possess, you become authentic. You realize that by being who you are, you are enough and will always be enough. I wish my dad knew he was enough, and that he didn't have to do anything extra. My gut instinct tells me he was trying to make his supervisors at work happy with the job he was on, and he put too much pressure on satisfying them that he forgot to satisfy himself. Whether that's true or not, I will never know but I knew my father and I knew how he did things. He wouldn't stop until a job was to his perception of perfection, which made everything he did incredibly well done.

Prayer is a balance of being still and conversing with God then knowing when to take action. You ask him for guidance and then open your ears to listen. There is a voice inside you telling you that you are meant for greatness, but when your opportunities come are you willing to move your feet? Maybe God is asking you to do something you don't want to do. Regardless, you need to do it, because on the other side of what you are supposed to do, there is a life that is so much more than you could ever imagine.

What is something you know you are supposed to do but because of a lack of faith you choose to ignore it? You can make excuses, or you can make a legacy, but you can't have both. It doesn't work like that and it never will work like that. You can see every situation as preparation for what's next or you can see it as just another day. You can go through the motions with putting little thought into what you are doing or step up and make a difference. Again, the choice is yours. You can train your mind through self-discipline, give yourself commands and then follow through with them. Listen to your conscious and then go do what needs to be done.

For over a year, I heard the word "write" in my mind. God was continuously telling me to write but I made excuses and I wasn't doing it. I would say I'm too tired, or that I didn't want to because I would rather watch Netflix or thumb around on social media. I was being selfish, and I wasn't thinking about praying with my feet. I was comfortable and life was fairly easy, but God kept poking at me, saying "write." I will never be able to avoid God's persistence because He is all-knowing and since He is all-knowing, He is nudging me towards everything that is going to give me a greater life. He wants me to be better today than yesterday and He wants me to be better tomorrow than today. He has something incredible planned for me in this life. He has the exact same plan for you as well, just open your ears and your heart. Move your feet when you need to act and fold your hands when you need to be still. Both forms of prayer are necessary and when you learn to balance them, you reach new levels of greatness.

Read through Ecclesiastes 3:1-22 and understand there is a time for everything, and God's timing is perfect. It is always perfect, but it is our imperfection and lack of faith that puts God's timing on delay. God gave you a soul to understand that there is perfection inside of you. You don't fail by making mistakes, you fail by quitting and giving up. There are many times God is willing to hand you everything you have ever wanted, but then you quit acting and God assumes that you don't really want what you thought you wanted. Your actions are not lined up with your prayers. There is a disconnect between what you say with folded hands and how you move your feet. So, when you pray, know that God is ready to give you the things you desire. All you have to do is show Him that what you desire is not only going to serve you, but also those around you.

Piece 11: Living in Balance with God

God has designed this world so perfectly that if you take the time to understand and study how to balance your mind, body and spirit, then life begins to flow with much more ease. When you learn to live in harmony with God's plan and if you are humble enough to recognize that God is preparing you for what is next, you will find purpose and fulfillment.

This means that you might have to go through some growing pains. It also means that you might have to battle through tough times to rejoice in greatness. However, you can make anything easier by using discipline, knowing what you want and then going after it. You are always creating habits in your life. Whether or not those habits are benefiting you and your quality of life is something that only you can answer for yourself.

Here are a few questions to keep in mind. Are your habits making your dreams become more of a reality? Is what you are doing every day getting you closer to what you really want? Do you feel like your life is getting a little better every day?

Dreams are simply illusions without the willingness to act. They stay dreams if you stay in your comfort zone. It's when you know you need to act that drives you. It doesn't matter what you need to do, you just go do it. It's when you realize that failings in life only happen when you give up and stop trying. I know I've mentioned that a few times, but you must rewire your mindset. There is always something to be learned from every experience and situation in your life. It is very possible you have had things happen in your life that didn't work out how you wanted them to at the time they happened. Although, what if you started saying to yourself, "Everything that happens to me in my life is what I needed to become the person God wants me to be."

I'm not saying you need tragedies in your life for it to be successful, but adversity can train you to be more resilient. It gives you a perspective on what should truly be valued in the world. You can put yourself through adversity simply by exercising and working out. That is the best way to start learning how to be comfortable feeling uncomfortable, and your body will love it.

It's something I put into practice in my own life. I set my alarm for 4:40 AM and I've trained myself to jump out of bed and immediately start moving. It's actually more of a slide out of bed, mamma bear needs her sleep. A ten to fifteen-minute run followed by yoga, stretching, or lifting. I do this to wake up my mind and win the first battle of the day, the battle of the bed. Then I spend the next 20 to 25 minutes in prayer/meditation/reflection. I tell myself that I am always enough and that I don't have to identify myself with titles associated with my job, home or personal life. I tell myself there is nothing I have to prove to anyone. Then the next 20 to 25 minutes, depending on how well my three-year-old is sleeping, I am learning something and crafting my skills. So before 6 AM I have already taken action to improve my body, soul and mind. This helps me balance personal, family, and work time. I've learned to feel when I am out of balance in life and I have learned a keen sense of what to do to get back in balance.

Through my intuition, which is God's voice talking to me, I get ideas on what I should presently be doing. Then it is up to me to listen and follow through with God's suggestions. I am still improving on taking action because my paradigms want to pull me back. However, I can honestly say I've never regretted a time when I have followed the advice of my intuition. I feel my purpose, I live my mission and I discover my desires when I make the choice to follow my intuitive hunches. You have that ability as well, you just need to choose to practice and develop it.

It took me a long time to want to trust my intuition and trust that good things were coming because of my unwillingness to listen. My dad's suicide was one of my first experiences with intuition and therefore left me not wanting to listen to that guiding voice. This caused an imbalance in my life that would force me to be nervous in my decision making, and I would often overthink my decisions. It also caused me to be timid because I didn't have the confidence in myself to go for the things I wanted. Eventually, I got tired of not winning and I realized that overthinking was exhausting my energy. I knew there had to be more and that I could do more, but I had to trust more. I had to trust my intuition and I had to believe that I could overcome my situation. That's when I discovered the importance of a growth mindset.

Piece 12: Growth Over Fixed

The two words that irk me the most in the English language are when I hear people say, "I can't." It is like nails on a chalkboard when I hear people say those words. Then it is normally followed up with some excuse of why they can't do it. The truth is whether you say, "I can" or "I can't," you're right. The difference is people who say, "I can" use determination, perseverance, and willpower. "I can" people are the problem solvers in our society and make the impossible possible, which is what we need more of in our society. Those who say "I can't" are the ones who keep impossibility alive. When you say, "I can't," what you fail to understand is that this is holding you back from your truest potential. I'd rather hear "I don't want to" than "I can't," because at least when you say,

"I don't want to" you still believe that you can. It is just something that you are making the choice not to do.

I have been in many situations where I didn't want to do something, but I needed to do it anyway. I learned this very quickly after having children. I realized that there were things that needed to be done and it was up to me to get it done. It didn't really matter if I wanted to do them or not. For example, getting up multiple times at night, changing diapers, waiting in the doctor's office and the list goes on. Simply knowing what you need to do can get you to take action and fight through what you don't want to do

You may have been conditioned in school to have a fixed mindset, mostly because of how you were probably graded. You might associate failing with negativity as opposed to an opportunity for growth. There may have been times where you felt pressure from parents and others to make certain grades, and you got fixated on what grade you received on a test. You couldn't care less if you learned anything, you just wanted to know what grade you got. If you are like me, you cram information in at the last second hoping to get a grade good enough to make your parents proud of you. Many times, I feel like most of us were motivated to get good grades because of parent expectations or to stay eligible for an extracurricular activity. It wasn't necessarily because we wanted the grade for ourselves. We were doing it for someone or something else, which conditions external motivation. I know that's not everyone, but I would say it is a sizable majority, especially for those of us who went through school in the United States.

When you learn with a fixed mindset you don't truly process what you are learning. You are simply memorizing for the test and then within about two days, you have forgotten almost everything you just learned. Then you graduate high school or college and think you don't have to learn anymore, but the reality is the learning has just begun. The truth is either you keep getting better or you will get passed up in our adulthood. Those who choose to continually improve themselves, learn balance and believe they can always get better at finding success because they are ok with failing. The best of the best have failed the most but, through that process, they figured out ways to improve things.

Often in school, you only get one chance at taking a test, and there are rarely any second chances or opportunities to learn what you did wrong. It is as if you just need to accept it as is and move on. No wonder test anxiety is a thing. What you don't realize is that the grade you get on a test is telling you what state of mind you were in during that test. If you were given the opportunity to take the test again with the same concepts and different questions, your score would increase more times than not. Then that improvement should be praised because the goal should be growth.

A growth mindset encourages learning by doing and then doing it better the next time. It encourages the concept of failing forward by giving your best effort, then trying again to improve based upon your last exam. If you can learn to develop a growth mindset, you would recognize that learning never stops regardless of what grade you are in at school or even how old you are. I want to reiterate that the most successful people in the world have developed a keen understanding that failure is leading them to their goal. Every time they fail, they think about how they can make it better and they keep trying until they get it right. Michael Jordan will tell you that he failed his way into success. He would say things like, "I have failed over and over again, and that is how I succeeded." He didn't let the outside world tell him that he wasn't good enough, he just kept his vision of what he wanted and went for it.

Figure out what you can do to get 1% better every day. Small daily steps lead to big leaps in the future. However, improving 1% each day means there needs to be 100% effort. It doesn't matter what activity you are doing, giving your best is required in order to grow. Think about that for a second, if you commit to improving your mind, body, and spirit 1% each day, you will be over three and a half times better as a person in one year. How much better would our world be if we all lived by the motto, "100 to 1". 100 to 1, meaning that it takes 100% effort to get 1% better every day. Try it yourself for 66 days. According to Robin Sharma, a life coach for professional athletes and CEOs of some of the top companies in the world, this is how long it takes to develop a new habit. Take note of how much will change in your life over that period of 66 days. I can almost guarantee it will get you to a point where you will get agitated if you skip learning for a day, because you remember how it feels and how much better your days go when you make a point to learn. Fix your eyes on growth and know that failure is just the blueprint leading you to greater things.

Piece 13: A Woman's Influence

Women can have significant influence on men's behavior. They can drive you insane or they can lift you up to places you never thought possible. They can bring you to new heights and at the same time make your life miserable. Choosing encouraging and uplifting women to be around is essential to a man's success. They can get you out of your comfort zone, challenge you to take risks and see a much different perspective. More importantly, finding the right woman to marry can literally change the course of your life. This is what happened to me during my last semester of college.

I was student teaching, so I wasn't on campus very much, but I spent a decent amount of time at the Catholic ministry designed for college students on Missouri State's campus. Go

Bears! I met so many amazing people there but, most importantly, it is where I met my wife, Mary. I had seen her around and she caught my eye a few times, but I had never really had the chance to talk to her. That all changed one night when me and a group of friends went to the Mud Lounge in downtown Springfield. I intentionally decided to sit next to her and try to get to know her. I felt those initial feelings of attraction immediately as I started talking to her. It was the perfect way to get to know her. We were with a big group of people. We all knew each other, which made it easy for Mary and I to talk and hang out.

I worked up the courage to ask her if she would like to exchange numbers, and she said "Yeah, sure!" I was trying to play it cool, but I was doing some major fist-pumping in my mind. I didn't know what it would lead to, but it was a boost of confidence I needed. I drove home sitting up a little taller, and the most excited I had been in a long time. Then, as I am pulling into my driveway, my phone starts ringing. Who was calling me at 1:00 am? It was her! "Wow, that didn't take long." I thought. I answered with the classic, "Hey what's up? Long-time no see" phrase. Turns out she was simply calling to let me know that I had a shirt hanging out of the trunk of my car as I drove away. I went from hero to zero very quickly, basically the opposite of Hercules, but she thought it was quite humorous.

It is a funny little story now that we have been together for over ten years, but at the time it was quite the roller coaster of going from excitement to embarrassment. You always want that perfect moment when you meet someone who you have an attraction to. You want to give the impression that you have your life together and that you are heading in the right direction. Maybe though, it was my imperfection and goofy moment that was the gateway for her to feel comfortable around me.

I look back at that memory as God teaching me that you don't have to come across as perfect. In fact, coming across as perfect is very intimidating to many people and that moment helped break the ice for future conversations. It was a good laugh for sure, and something that we still joke about. The fact that I was able to laugh at myself during that situation helped her realize that I didn't take life too seriously. Fast forward three years and I am asking her to marry me; fast forward another five years we are married with two beautiful and healthy boys. If you can laugh at yourself when funny things happen to you, like a shirt hanging out of your car, that makes people so much more comfortable around you.

I couldn't imagine spending life with anyone else, she is truly my best friend and her support means everything to me. Sometimes you just need someone to come along in your life that believes in you. She also showed me that she had confidence in me and when I told her that I needed to write this book. She said, "I can't wait to read it!" It is amazing what you can do when you have authentic support from your spouse. She also helps me think about my choices and decisions. She always seems to ask the right questions to encourage my thought processes. Her questions seem to help guide me to the next essential step. I believe God is using her to check my motives and my intentions. Why do I have these desires I have? Why do I have these lofty goals? Are they making an impact on others, not just myself?

We need someone like that in our lives. We need someone who will be direct but not demeaning. Someone to ask the tough questions to make sure the ideas and thoughts we are having are positively impacting humanity, not just ourselves. She helped me realize that what I want for myself, I also want for everyone else. That is what a spouse does. Simply by being who she is, she helps me dig a little deeper, check my intentions and take action. Sometimes she doesn't even have to say anything. Now, before I act, I am doing a better job of thinking. I am using my God-given mind to make an impact because when I look at my wife and children, I want to give them the best life possible.

One of the best things she did for me was help me learn how to get out of my comfort zone. We went to Europe twice after we got married. There was a time in my life where going on a plane gave me chills, much less flying across the ocean. I learned to love to travel because of her and I have a new appreciation for wine because when you go to Italy, the beer really isn't that good.

She has listened to me talk about my struggles with losing my dad and the affect it has had on me. She has been patient with me as I go through this lifelong process to discern and understand the meaning behind what happened with him. She has been my biggest supporter and has pushed me to expand my abilities beyond my perceived limitations. I can tell her when I had a day where I struggled more than usual, and she wraps her arms around me and gives me the most comforting hug in my time of need. God once again puts the right person in my life to meet my needs. I've learned that all I need to have in life is faith and patience then allow God to show me his plans as they unfold a little more every day.

Here is another recommendation, marry someone who will love you through and through regardless of what happens. Every day, I try and ask myself, "how can I be more helpful to Mary?" I know the more we help each other the better our marriage will get. I also recognize that my boys need to see an example of how a man treats his wife. There are little eyes watching every move I make. I am their perception of the world right now, which is something I have always wanted. It's a constant reminder that I need to be showing them how to love another person. Every day is an opportunity to be an example for them to follow, so they can live their best life when they become men.

The greatest role in my life is not being a teacher, coach, speaker, or writer. My greatest role in life is being a great husband to Mary and being an involved father to my boys, Louis and Noah. I try to have a positive attitude every day and am so thankful for the opportunity to be a husband and father. I try to see what good can come out of every situation. It is tough to think like this sometimes, especially that time when I was pooped on, it was 20 degrees outside, and I forgot an extra set of clothes so had to run back home. However, I've now built the habit of continually asking myself, "What is the good that will come from this?" Then I have the faith that life is getting better and better.

Looking for the positives takes some rewiring of thoughts, but it can become a habit with intentional application. The more it is practiced the more you do it without thinking twice. It becomes a habit when you get the life you've always dreamed of having. It becomes your reality. I was sent through the valley of losing my father to suicide, but I kept pushing forward. If I would have given up, I probably wouldn't have met Mary and I definitely wouldn't have had the chance to marry her. Keep your head up and know that God is putting the right people in your life at the right moments when you need them.

Piece 14: Victims Lose and Winners Choose

Regardless of what happens in life, you always have a choice on how to look at any situation. When you choose to act like a victim of your situation, you will always lose. I could have easily done that in my situation with my dad. Honestly, the first six months to a year afterward I did occasionally want people to feel bad for me. I associated people feeling bad for me as a way for people to show they still cared about me.

Certain days, like birthdays and holidays, will always be tougher than others, but there were some days that I just wanted people to feel bad for me. What I didn't think about was if I want people to simply feel bad for me, what kind of relationships am I forming with my friends and family? Why would people want to be around me if I am negative and mopey? It took me a while to figure this out, but eventually I snapped out of my funk, smelled the roses and thought, "My attitude right now isn't making my life better." I finally understood that feeling sorry for myself was not helping my situation.

Playing the victim is very enticing and it feeds into the origin of your mind. You are wired for negativity because that's how humans survived thousands of years ago. However, we have evolved as a species to the point where thinking negative is now what holds us back more than anything. When all you want to do is think negatively and look for people to feel bad for you, you're going to lose. People are less likely to help those who wallow in self-pity because those who pity themselves do not help themselves. Acting like a victim is a great way to limit your potential, bury your talents, and fall in line with the masses.

It's one thing to feel the pain of a situation; this allows you to start the healing process to learn and grow. It's another thing to feel the pain of the situation and allow it to defeat you then use it as an excuse to give up on yourself. Feeling the pain of a situation is absolutely healthy. Feel it deeply and to the core, but then allow yourself to heal. Allow yourself to forgive and take something away from the situation that will make you a better person. Your life will look much different if you learn how to handle painful situations. There is an opportunity in every situation to make you a better person. What if everything you are going through right now was supposed to happen to you so you can help someone else get through similar struggles?

I know it might not be easy or enjoyable and it takes great intention to think positive in difficult situations. However, asking yourself questions like, "What good will come from this?" and "How is this going to make me a better person?" will bring you much more peace of mind. This way of thinking has been a learning curve for me. There have been many times when I've been faced with decisions and I would think of the worst-case scenario. What I have learned to do now is also consider the best possible scenario. When I have tried this way of thinking, good things started happening and drew me toward those best-case scenarios I had in my mind. Either way you look when making a decision, keep a positive perspective and use your intuition to guide you. Your gut feeling is right almost all the time if you trust it.

We need fewer victims in our world and more modern-day warriors. A modern-day warrior is resilient and doesn't allow failure to give them a pass to quit on their dreams. We shouldn't dismiss feeling sad or upset. It's healthy to cry when a situation has caused you pain or grief but remember to also smile and laugh. Don't let the world or your circumstances steal your joy. You can make an impact on the world if you can get yourself to think and see the good that is coming. I choose to believe that my life is getting better and better every day. The past is what it is, and the future will be what it will be. I know that I can create my future by what I am doing in the present and giving it all I have. I know that by being present, I can make an impact on others and I can have the most fulfilling balanced life possible. I know this because I tried to play the victim, and when I got tired of losing, I decided there must be a better way. I hate losing anyway, so when I asked myself "why do I keep playing this role?" I didn't have a good answer and all I could come up with were excuses. It was the perfect time to change my thought process and my attitude.

I want to win every day because I know if I win today that sets me up to have more success tomorrow. I always attempt to choose actions that I think will make me a better person. Every success is a building block for the next opportunity. Brick by brick the house is built. Challenges can disguise themselves as opportunities for growth. I do everything I can to keep myself humble and grounded because every person I come across knows something that I don't know. I've learned that nothing should be taken for granted and that I should be cherishing even the smallest moments. What I have today, I have earned and what I will have in the future will be because I choose discipline. I stay true to myself and I do not let others' criticism or pessimism sway me. I reject those opinions, tell them thanks for sharing and move on. Incorporating gratitude helps me raise my awareness of how good my life is, keeps me from playing the victim card and reminds me of all the good that's coming my way.

Piece 15: Autopilot Good Choices

L ife can be very simple, but we make it so complicated at times. Every day is an opportunity to be more, do more, and learn more. We can become more through making choices that will benefit us. It is important to learn from circumstances where we had good intentions, but the result played out a little differently than what you initially had in mind. I struggled for years knowing I had to fully forgive my dad but knowing it and doing it were two different things. I had every intention of doing it, but until I finally made the choice to forgive, I was holding myself back.

When you get to a point where you continue to make choices that are beneficial, your life will continuously improve. When you think life is getting better and better and your choices reflect that in your daily actions, then that is what will happen. If you think negative and think about the worst-case scenarios, then that is probably what will happen as well.

The choices you make are rooted deep into what you truly believe. Everything you choose to do is based on a belief you have about yourself or about how you perceive the circumstances around you. If you believe you are healthy, you will choose to exercise and eat foods you know are good for you. It doesn't mean you can't partake in a dessert or a favorite food occasionally, but what it does mean is that you know how to limit yourself on things that hold little to no nutritional value.

When you choose to learn and improve yourself every day, then you improve your quality of life and you make life better for those who are a part of your life. Everyone wants to be around people who give off positive energy, who smile and laugh. Life isn't that serious most of the time, and it deserves to be enjoyed. Some of the things you might get worked up and stressed over probably won't even matter within the next year, month, week or even the next day. Next time, when you feel yourself getting worked up about something, simply ask, "Is this going to matter next week, next month or next year?" More times than not, you will probably say no.

Why choose to put so much energy into those things? Do yourself a favor and let it go. I understand there will be times where grieving will be necessary and there will be times that will challenge you, but if you can understand that every perceived bad situation has an equal and opposite good situation, then you can shift your focus onto the positive. When challenging times surface, think of all the good you have.

Choose to be thankful for what you have been given and stop comparing yourself to others. There is no reason to look at what someone else has and wish you had it. Be happy for them, and know your time is coming. If you develop positive mental chatter by saying things like, "Hey I have it pretty good, and I am choosing to make my life better!" You will make choices that improve the quality of your life. Exercise your body and mind, pray with gratitude, and don't let the outside world get you off track. It is a battle of the mind. Remember, the mind is wired towards negativity. However, you can change your thoughts and filter what you believe. Think about this for a second: Why do you think the news is so depressing to watch? It is because that's what gets the ratings up. I stopped watching the news a long time ago because I never felt good after hearing what it had to say. I choose to take the negative out of my life and focus on the positive.

I had every excuse in the book to choose other things to try and fill up the grief in my heart from my father's suicide. However, I chose to go to college, and I chose to be around people who I have had success in things l wanted for myself. I decided that I still had my life to live and that I needed to make the most of what I had. It wasn't easy leaving for college a little over a year after my dad passed away, but I wanted a degree and

I wanted to go my own way for a while. I wanted to experience the unfamiliar so I could start to make my own path. It was met with resistance at first as my mom did not want me to go at the time. She wanted me to stay close to home. I can't blame her; I would probably feel the same way when I look at it from her point of view. Now, when she and I talk about that decision, we talk about how it was what we both needed.

Choosing to go to Missouri State gave me not only a degree but also the confidence in knowing I can still have a good life. It was there where I built lifelong friendships and most importantly it was there where I met my wife. If I would have done what everyone else wanted me to do, I don't know if I can say with certainty that I would have the same quality of life. In fact, I know I wouldn't. I still had to move forward even though I felt left behind. I had to find out for myself that there was something more than pain in my adult life. I had to find out who I was without the direct influence of my family and lifelong friends telling me what they thought was best for me.

Sometimes making the right choices are the most difficult. I like asking myself two questions when faced with a decision. What are the short-term benefits and what are the long-term benefits? I want every choice I make to somehow improve my life. This takes a lot of practice and requires choices to be made that I may not want to do, but I know I won't regret doing them. The key is making the right choices a habit and acting immediately before your mind talks you out of things. Almost like putting yourself on autopilot. For example, you know you need to clean the dishes, but you hate unloading the dishwasher. The more you sulk and focus on what you hate doing the longer it will take to get it done. However, if you see the dishes that need to be done, flip on your inner autopilot. Keep it simple and just do it, like Nike has been telling us for years. The dishes will be done, and you can move on to something more enjoyable.

If you decide to put making good choices on autopilot, you will love the results you get. It doesn't mean you will want to do everything you need to do, but what it does mean is that you will be glad you made the choice to do those things. You will reap the benefits of acting on the choices you know you need to do. You will find success quickly if you learn to autopilot those beneficial choices of healthy mind, soul and body.

If you desire, take these pieces of wisdom and implement them gradually into your life. You can be the difference; know that you have more to give than you ever thought possible. When you weave positivity and faith together it doesn't matter what you do because you will impact peoples' lives. You will make a difference. You can weave your thoughts together by always believing that something better is headed your way. Your opportunity is coming! Be ready and willing to take advantage of it. Finally, become a better version of yourself every day. Have a goal of being the best at what you are doing right now. This way you will be ready to open the door when God comes knocking with your next opportunity.

A Crescendo of Joy and Thankfulness
(A Modern Day Citation)

I am so joyous and thankful for the people God has placed in my life. My wife and sons are a true blessing. They inspire me to go for greatness and continue to be better than before. I am so thankful for the support of my loving wife, Mary, who encourages the work that I do because she understands my mission and my purpose. Everyone deserves a spouse like that. I, in turn, will continually support her as she fulfills her purpose and mission.

I am so joyous and thankful for my mother, sisters, and grandmother, who all taught me how to be strong. My mom and grandma never complained, they just kept moving forward. They set the example of knowing what needs to be done and then getting it done. They are also extremely giving and loving. They are always helpful, willing to listen and give sound advice. My sisters also kept pushing forward when times were tough.

Each of us persevered and we are creating amazing families that cultivate our family joy.

I am so joyous and thankful for Daniel, Ben, and Allan who are my three closest friends from high school. I have so many incredible memories with those guys and a connection that always picks up right where we left off, regardless of how long it's been since we've seen or talked with each other.

I am so joyous and thankful for Tyler, Chase, Seth and Garet. These were the guys in college that turned into the brothers I never had growing up. We were always authentic with each other, and we always had so many great times. We built our faith together and we were always there for each other as we went through the complexities of figuring out how to be men.

I am so joyous and thankful to Jeff and Tim. Their example helped keep me on the right path because I saw what they had, and I wanted that for myself. They had confidence, passion, charisma and a dedication to their own life to be the best version of themselves every day. Their compassion towards me will always be remembered as I pay it forward to the lives I plan on impacting.

I am so joyous and thankful to my Godparents Marvin and Debbie. They were there for me when I needed them the most after my dad's passing. They spent a lot of time with me making sure I was okay. Now I can say I am better than I have ever been before, and I strive to continue to get better every day.

I am so joyous and thankful for Mary, Ralph, and Jenna who read, formatted and edited this book. They are so talented with words and grammar. It is because of them that I was able to get this book finished quicker than I ever expected!

I am so joyous and thankful for Melody, who also edited this book. She gave me my first job opportunity and she believed in me from the very beginning of my career. Because of her willingness to take a chance on me, I have built an amazing life here in Kansas City. Those six years were a great foundation for my career as an educator, coach, writer, and speaker.

I am so joyous and thankful for the work of Wallace Wattles, Napoleon Hill, Bob Proctor and Vishen Lakhiani. As well the quotes from Thomas Edison, Michael Jordan, and Robin Sharma. I have grown so much through studying their content and applying the action steps they recommend to not only become successful, but impactful as well.

Finally, I am so joyous and thankful for Jim. His presence has made such a huge impact in my life and he taught me what it means to be a coach. He taught me that life is much more than just W's and L's or X's and O's. It's about preparation and impact. His knowledge of the game and his willingness to help me as I got started on my coaching journey helped me find success. Once again God brought him in my life at the perfect time and was exactly the mentor I needed.

About the Author

Growing up in Taos, Missouri, Jason was raised in a loving family that gave him every chance to succeed. His parents were supportive and provided everything this 17-year-old boy desired. That is until his life changed forever on May 8, 2003, when his dad unexpectedly died from suicide and left him, his mother and two younger sisters behind.

Through hard work, dedication and a strong faith, Jason is now a certified teacher, accomplished basketball coach, and up and coming author and motivational speaker. His dedication to positively impacting the lives of those around him inspired the hashtag #ACT2IMPACT which serves as a reminder that we all can make a difference.

Jason is a dedicated and loving husband and father who strives to help others overcome the lasting effects of suicide. Jason sits on the board for the USSI (United Suicide Survivors International) alongside world renowned entrepreneur and innovator in social change and suicide prevention, Dr. Sally Spencer Thomas. Along with others around the world, they are raising awareness that suicide doesn't stop life from get worse, it eliminates the opportunity for life to improve.

Made in the USA
Columbia, SC
07 March 2020